MW01065983

The Ultimate Survival Guide
For TEACHERS

*An inspirational and hilarious handbook for
the world's most misunderstood wilderness*

Scotty Hicks & Rob Kuban

"May the odds be ever in your favor."
     - Effie Trinket (The Hunger Games)

S*urvival.* In an age when we enjoy the comfiest, coziest, and most controllable standard of living, we have an insatiable obsession with survival. From the early days of *Survivor* and *Lost*, to more recent hits like *Man vs. Wild, The Walking Dead,* and *The Hunger Games,* we have a peculiar preoccupation with facing raw encounters in the untamed wilderness.

Maybe the fascination stems from questioning our own chances if we were facing similar circumstances: *Would I make it?* Could *I* survive in the wild? What if a meteor wiped out my very way of life, and I had nothing but a Swiss army knife and faded memories of MacGyver's highlight reel? Would I make it? What if zombies took over the world and my only friend was a German Shepherd named Sam? Could I do it? *Do I have what it takes?*

While we might question our own odds, one thing is certain: Former British Special Forces member and survivalist Bear Grylls has what it takes. From chewing on animal carcasses to repelling down a cliff with a rope made out of tree bark to fighting off dehydration by drinking his own urine, Bear proves that he is willing to do *whatever* is necessary to survive. It doesn't take long into an episode of *Man vs. Wild* before you ask yourself: "Is there anything that Bear Grylls *wouldn't* do?!?" We believe there is...

Bear Grylls wouldn't wait for someone else to come fix his problems—he knows that *he* is his best shot at making it out alive. He wouldn't gripe about the lack of available resources in his current location—he forces himself to make the most of what he has. He wouldn't vent to the rocks and trees about how much easier it was to survive twenty years ago—he spends his energy *in*venting solutions appropriate for his particular situation. He wouldn't approach any task halfheartedly—he passionately pursues survival *as if his life*

Acknowledgments and Thanks

Scotty

To my wife, Joy, and two children, Lincoln and Bella, for *giving me purpose and love on a daily basis.*

To the McCampbells and everyone like them, *who made me believe in myself.*

To my students, for making me believe that *the future is not bleak.*

Rob

To Jordan, my wonderful wife, *for always loving and supporting me.*

To Zachary and Ansley, my incredible children, *for teaching me what students never could.*

To Mrs. Shipley, Coach Rush, and Mr. Davis (Oak Ridge High School), *for inspiring me to become a teacher.*

To Dr. Baker, Dr. Rutledge, and Dr. Ellington (University of Tennessee at Chattanooga) *for helping to shape my classroom.*

Table of Contents

THRIVING
Leaving a legacy that goes beyond learning

Introduction

THE STORIES YOU ARE ABOUT TO READ
ARE ALL TRUE.

ONLY THE NAMES HAVE BEEN CHANGED
TO PROTECT THE INNOCENT...
AND THE NOT SO INNOCENT!

Getting lost in the wilderness

"Mr. Kuban?"

It was my (Rob) first year teaching, and I started the day confident that I had created a dynamic lesson. We were discussing how the Continental soldiers, after spending decades clashing with Native Americans, approached the fight for independence from Britain with an entirely different concept of warfare. Despite some humiliating losses, Britain often held fast to traditional tactics; whereas, we Americans seemed willing to do whatever it took to win our new found dream of a nation ruled by "We the people." *I was firing on all cylinders.* How could a student *not* be entranced by such a powerful and engaging lesson?!? I was wrapping things up, beaming with pride for such polished pedagogy, when a student interrupted with a question:

"Mr. Kuban?"

"Yes."

"Did people ever use snakes in war?"

"Excuse me?"

"You know, did people ever use snakes in war?"

"Um...uh...I don't understand the question."

"I was watching this movie last night called *Anaconda,* and it had this HUGE snake in it, and it killed a BUNCH of people. So I was wondering if people ever, you know, trained snakes to fight in wars."

[Long silence]

"Ah...no. People have never trained snakes to fight for them in times of war."

"Well, they *should,* that snake was scary!"

"Oh yea! I saw it too," another student piped in. Within seconds the entire class jumped into a passionate discussion of *Anaconda*, snakes, horror movies, and pretty much anything *except* the Revolutionary War. First block.

The next class didn't go much better. I made it halfway through my lesson before a student interjected with his own unique commentary:

"Hey Mr. Kuban."

"Yes."

"Why did you buy those shoes?"

"What? What are you talking about? The shoes that I am wearing?"

"Yea, why did you buy them?"

"I...needed a pair of shoes??? I am not sure why you are asking me."

"Well, they are ugly. I just thought you should know."

If I thought first block had a lot to say about snakes, it *paled in comparison* to my students' opinions of my wardrobe's deficiencies! Every fashion faux pas dating back to the first day of school was brought to my direct attention. Second block.

Finally, I had planning to re-group. I shook it all off, tried to learn from my mistakes, and got ready to hit it out of the park in my final class. They showed up, class started, and before I could even get the lesson off the ground a student puked up and down the center aisle of my classroom floor. The janitor showed up, spread the infamous "saw dust" stuff on the floor (that some how seems to make it smell even *worse*), and we were forced to finish "class" in the stairwell.

On the way home, I wasn't sure if I should laugh or cry. My mind wandered. I tried to remember what exactly I was thinking when I chose to be a teacher. It wasn't until I saw the blue flashing lights in my rear-view mirror that I realized I had driven straight through a speed trap. *Forty-eight in a thirty-five*. The icing on the cake.

2

We don't need any help getting lost in the wilderness of modern education. Kind of like gaining weight or going broke, we seem fully capable of getting ourselves into a mess without much assistance. That being said, bookstores are full of books to get our abs ready for the beach or pick investments to secure our nest egg, but there seems to be no book with pure and simple *pragmatic* advice for teachers. *We decided to change that.*

~

About the Authors

Between the two of us, we have experience teaching in *seven* different schools in *four* different systems. We've taught in classes that range from an urban school in the middle of a big city to a rural school in a small town, and from high performing areas to low performing areas. In all of these settings, our students have shown a substantial amount of success when staring down the beast, the infamous "king of the educational jungle," *the standardized test.* We don't have all the answers, we aren't perfect teachers, and we have by no means tamed the vast wilderness of American education (be wary of anyone who says they have!). But we have learned a great deal of hard-earned academic wisdom from our wide range of experiences and are convinced it will serve a teacher well no matter where or what they teach.

Scotty Hicks:

Scotty has served our country in two battlefronts, Operation Iraqi Freedom and the classroom. Within his teaching career, he has received the P.T.A. National Lifetime Achievement Award (2006), was selected as the WBIR-TV Educator of the Week (2009) and the V.F.W. Tennessee Teacher of the Year (2011). He has been chosen as a U.S. House of Representatives *House Fellow* (2009) and a Horace

3

Mann *Abraham Lincoln Fellow* (2011). His own children recently placed 1st (for the 6th year in a row!) in the "Smartest, cutest, and most likely to rule the world" contest staged annually in his home by their mother.

Rob Kuban:
Rob has been selected as the Tennessee Council for the Social Studies Middle School Teacher of the Year (2010), East Tennessee Historical Society Teacher of the Year (2009), and Outstanding Teacher of American History by the Daughters of the American Revolution historical society (2012). His students have won national recognition for their work in the Junior American Citizen's contest and regional recognition in the VFW's Patriot's Pen Essay contest. He is also the founder and current president of the educational alliance *T.A.E.C.P.* (Teachers Against Empty Coffee Pots).

4

SURVIVING

Learning how to lead your classroom instead of leave your classroom

"You're either in or you're out."

- Daniel Ocean

There is a scene in *Ocean's 11* that is reminiscent of education. Daniel Ocean recruits Linus with a simple question:

"You're either in or you're out. *Right now.*"

"What is it?"

"It's a plane ticket—a job offer."

No details, no information, and no chance to back out, just a question: Are you in or are you out? What's it going to be? *Right now.* Every teacher can relate to this ultimatum—a certain "sign on the dotted line" before you *really* know what exactly you are signing up for. As new teachers, *we merged into the fast lane of a large educational interstate during rush hour with a "student driver" sticker in the window—getting into the thick of things before really knowing how to drive.* Of course we all *thought* we could cruise our classroom down the academic freeway, but when the apple hit the fan, we all became a lot less certain. The following section is designed to help all teachers increase their odds of surviving not only their christening into the American classroom, but also their *career*.

Dirty Diapers
and Dirty Words

Chapter 1

Maintaining your sense of humor and remembering to have fun

To set this chapter off in the right direction, I (Rob) have decided to tell the story of a day when I made my student a "sandwich" he will never forget. I had a class that came straight from lunch in the cafeteria to my room (don't you *love* those classes!). Somewhere along the line some students in that class decided that they wanted to make me a sandwich (a gesture of their appreciation for all the wonderful lessons, I'm sure). But, it wasn't just any old sandwich. It was a jelly sandwich—two buns and every packet of jelly they could empty before the bell rang! Needless to say, I put it on the corner of my desk to eat "later." The following day I was presented with a chicken finger and mustard sandwich. Then, an orange sandwich, an apple sandwich, a hand sanitizer sandwich, and on, and on until the kids spent half of their lunch period trying to concoct the world's weirdest sandwich.

Every day, it made me smile as another sandwich went to the corner of my desk. About a month after all this began, the student ringleader of this whole insane operation did something rather remarkable. I told him I was proud of him and asked if there was anything I could do that would be an adequate reward. He smiled with a mischievous grin and said, "Yea, I want *you* to make *me* a sandwich!" The class roared. I laughed, and said I would make him a sandwich he would never forget.

Now the pressure was on. I had painted myself into a corner and had to deliver. The only problem was that I had

9

no clue what I was going to do. That evening as I was getting my daughter ready for bed, I folded up an explosively potent, foul, and overly full diaper and an evil scheme hatched in my mind. The following morning I grabbed two buns from our freezer and a spare, *clean* diaper.

Just before school, I filled the diaper to the brim with water (fully sanitary for all of you concerned parents!). I slid it in between two buns and there was my masterpiece, a "diaper sandwich" ready to go for sixth period. When class came, the gift was presented, and we all shared a great laugh. No one was quite sure *what* was inside the diaper, which only added to the hysteria.

We start with this story for one simple reason: As teachers, we can *never* lose our sense of humor. *It's easy to get frustrated by the regular doses of insanity that come with the territory of being a teacher, but we have the choice to let our students make us laugh.* It sounds like a simple choice, but day in and day out we have to fight the danger of letting our sense of humor dull towards our students and our profession.

Here are two goals that will help every teacher get to retirement with *a lot* better stories and a few less gray hairs:

Try to make your students laugh every day.
Allow your students to make you laugh every day.

I certainly have failed — and failed miserably — on one or both of these principles here and there in my career, but overall I try to remember these simple rules. My sixth period class that year will not soon forget the time that "Mr. Kuban made a diaper sandwich." I could have chosen to nip the sandwich making in the bud on the grounds of wasting food or some other responsible sounding excuse, but *I chose to let my students make me laugh.* And, I can't help but smile when I think that those guys spent half their lunch trying to figure out a new way to make me laugh.

While these two simple rules will help you navigate *predictable* circumstances with a sense of humor, any teacher knows that our profession is anything but a "controlled" environment. *All teachers know that plans rarely go according to plan.* What is that famous line? "The best laid plans of mice, men, and teachers." Something like that. This brings us to our *third* rule.

~

"Oh Fudddddddgggggggge! Only I didn't say 'fudge'. I said <u>the</u> word, the big one, the queen mother of dirty words."
                              - Ralphie (A Christmas Story)

I (Scotty) spent eleven years in the Army National Guard and spent some of that time serving active duty in Iraq. After returning home to my family and my teaching career, I wanted to expose my students to the sacrifices of the countless men and women who defend our freedom. To do so, I invited one of my fellow soldiers to my school to speak about some of his personal experiences in combat. I asked *him* specifically because he exemplifies the selfless sacrifice of our soldiers. When his first tour was over, he *volunteered* to serve a second one back to back. He is also a good friend of mine, and I knew the students would love him. He graciously agreed and all of my students were looking forward to the upcoming presentation.

When the day arrived, the auditorium was packed to the gills with over one hundred and fifty students, my head principal, a handful of parents, and at least half a dozen teachers. My friend, who had a reputation for using "colorful" vocabulary, was duly prepped to remember his audience. To be honest, I was a bit nervous that he might slip a small sample of the free flowing art form of cursing that the military is famous for into his presentation. After all, going from a combat zone to a middle school is anything but an easy transition!

However, when his presentation was complete, I was pleasantly surprised. He had been professional, articulate, and entertaining. When he asked if anyone had any questions, one usually timid student raised her hand and said, "What was one of the *weirdest* things that happened to you?" (Don't kids have the best questions!?!)

He paused, thought about it for a moment, and responded with excitement, "I don't need to tell you, I can *show* you!" He quickly started perusing through his laptop folders and mumbled that he was looking for a video clip. The auditorium was bursting with curiosity, and I felt a butterfly in my stomach as I began wondering what exactly was going to be broadcast on the large projector in the middle of the room.

"Ah, here it is!" he exclaimed.

The video started out rather tame, showing himself and two other soldiers leaning on a crate and eating MRE's (field food, Meals Ready, *or not so ready*, to Eat). Then suddenly a squirrel jumped off of the crate and onto his shoulder hoping to swipe a bite of some wonderful military chow! We all started laughing at the situation, and I felt my nerves begin to ease, *then it happened* – the big one, the queen mother of dirty words.

The audio from his video clip came blaring through the sound system: "WHAT THE _____??!!!" I will let you fill in the blank, and *all the other blanks* as three combat soldiers on active duty were attacked by a ravenous squirrel!

After the first expletive, my jaw (*and* one hundred and fifty students', *and* my head principal's, *and* the parents', *and* my co-workers') dropped to the floor faster than the squirrel jumped off the crate. The whole scenario plays back in my mind like a slow motion scene from *The Matrix*. I immediately began sprinting toward the speakers hoping to find mute before any more – what did I call it – free flowing art came through the speakers, but the damage had already been done. No less than three "big ones," three "queen mothers" had been dropped on the educational battlefield before the madness was stopped. For a moment, the auditorium fell deathly silent. *Then...*

Well think about it. This was a room full of a hundred and fifty 8th graders. This potentially could have been the greatest moment of their entire educational experience! They were laughing so hard, it took at least ten minutes to get them to calm down. When our speaker finally regained their attention, all he could say was: "I think that is enough questions for now." And the crowd went wild all over again!

Later I approached my principal afraid to look him in the eye, but when I was able to do so, guess what he was doing? *Smiling.* Mapping out a plan for damage control I'm sure, but smiling nonetheless.

To say that I had a few reasons to be stressed out at that moment would be the understatement of the century. First things first, I *wasn't* tenured. To be honest, I was convinced my job was on the line. In my mind, phone calls were being made to the newspapers, the superintendent was preparing to make a statement denouncing my teaching credentials, and my reputation was going to be scarred for life! Luckily, my principal quickly put my mind at ease. Everyone there knew it was a blunder — an honest mistake. My brother in arms had long forgotten what was stated in that video (though I am sure he will never forget again!).

In actuality, the only real results of that debacle were *numerous* entertaining conversations around dinner tables, classrooms, and of course, the faculty lounge. This incredibly stressful situation is now just an incredibly hilarious memory.

Any teacher that wants to survive in this profession without heavy medication, needs to take the following advice to heart:

Smile: In the grand scheme of things, many "stressful situations" are just hilarious memories in the making!

As a teacher, you can never forget to bring your sense of humor into your classroom. When you review vocabulary and a student defines "cartography" as "a person who takes pictures of cars," when a kid asks you if they speak French in France, when a you overhear a student say he is five foot twelve, and when an *8th* grader asks you half way through the year what the "A" in U.S.A. stands for, you *have* to maintain your sense of humor. Of course humorous situations in the classroom are one thing, but when the server goes down, the coffee pot is broken, Johnny forgot his homework *again*, the state changes legislation, or the kids are riding a sugar high the day after Halloween, *it's a different ballgame.*

The ups and downs of education can rock the boats of even the best teachers. *Just know that you are not alone.* The joys that accompany working with kids are occurring in classrooms across the globe. *Being a successful teacher is not so much about trying to eliminate stresses as it is learning how to navigate them, and one of the <u>best</u> stress management tools is a good sense of humor.* This doesn't mean you don't try to minimize stress, it simply means:

> *"In your life, expect some trouble,*
> *But when you worry, you make it double.*
> *Don't worry*
> *Be happy."*
> *- Bobby McFerrin*

Take a moment to think back over some of the experiences that this crazy profession has laid at your doorstep. What are some of your hilarious memories (now that you are looking *back* on them)? Thinking over some of your less than perfect experiences in education will help you keep things in perspective, and hopefully will remind you to *laugh*. If nothing else, it will remind you not to take yourself *too* seriously...which is where we would like to turn our attention next.

Laughing at yourself

"You know, Lloyd. Just when I think you couldn't possibly be any dumber, you go and do something like this...And TOTALLY REDEEM YOURSELF!"
- Harry (Dumb and Dumber)

There is one day at school we have been trying—with the aid of many therapists—to purge from our memories. The male teachers had been finagled into a "fashion show" fundraiser coordinated by the students and their health teachers to raise money for earthquake relief in Haiti. The only hitch—us men had to dress like, you guessed it, *women*. For myself (Rob), the fashion show wasn't nearly as embarrassing as purchasing my dress. At the local Goodwill store, I tried on a couple dresses until I found one that fit. I thought that I had done so discreetly, but any attempt at protecting my man pride was dashed on the rocks when my four year old son announced excitedly to the cashier and everyone in line: *"This is a dress for my daddy to wear to work!"* No saving face after something like that!

Despite doing a cat walk donning a floral dress in front of eight hundred screaming middle schoolers, Scotty is really the one to blame for the hours I have spent on a therapist's couch trying to forget that day. You see, Scotty considered the day a grand opportunity to get in touch with his "inner woman." He dressed up as Hannah Montana and performed—lip-syncing and break dancing—in front of the entire school. *It was a riot!* When he exited the gym floor sweating, we were all laughing and shaking our heads.

15

Then, he said something profound: "Hey, you can't embarrass me. I'm a teacher!" We all had a good laugh that day (*especially* the students), *and* we were able to raise over three thousand dollars to send to Haiti!

His statement is so true though. Any teacher will tell you: *A school is not a good place to work on your ego.* If you feel too good about yourself, more often than not you can count on your students to:

- point out the stains on your shirt (or *any* other deficiencies in your wardrobe)
- laugh when your voice cracks
- tell you that you say "like" a lot
- look bored to tears during a lesson you thought was fantastic
- let you know when you have a bad hair day
- tell you what their dad said about you
- remind you every time you forget something
- inform you when your room stinks
- inform you when your breath stinks
- inform you when *you* stink
- tell you that you have something in your teeth
- assure you that their parents' income is *much* higher than yours
- correct your grammar on a regular basis
- tell you what their mom said about you
- point out that they are taller than you
- make fun of your accent
- tell you that they think you are weird
- and on, and on, and on

Can *you* think of some other things to add to this list? We know it may not be quite as humorous at the exact moment a student tells you your clothes look funny, laughs at your salary, or asks why you have a big red bump on your forehead, but we hope that in the big picture you can learn to laugh at yourself. If not, you might just be strung a little too tight be a teacher.

If you want make it in this career, you have to laugh at yourself... frequently.

Practicing this skill on a regular basis actually helps students laugh at themselves as well, and creates a classroom environment that gives everyone a little room to breathe. In short, *it keeps us all from getting too serious and reminds us that nothing in life functions as smoothly as we all wish our classroom would.*

In order to emphasize this all too important skill, we decided to take a few cracks at ourselves before our students get another chance. We stole a page from Jeff Foxworthy's notebook and put our own unique twist on it. Take a few moments to practice the art of learning how to laugh at yourself.

You might be a teacher if...

- You've ever asked complete strangers to spit out their gum.
- You still get little giddy when any bit of snow is in the forecast.
- You've ever been forced to hold an impromptu parent conference at Wal-Mart, the post office, church, the soccer field, or in a public restroom.
- You've mastered the act of pretending to know someone's name who obviously knows yours.
- You have a sixth sense for "Free Food."
- You regularly correct people's grammar in conversations (or at least want to!).
- You've said things to copy machines that would make a sailor blush.
- You've ever gone somewhere on vacation to learn more about what you teach.

- Your family has a seating chart at the dinner table.
- You can remember two hundred kids' names but can't remember where you put your keys.
- You have a secret stash of school supplies...at your house.
- You think nothing of correcting the behavior of other people's children in public.
- You've ever had to change doctors because a former student took your blood pressure, weighed you, and asked you to strip down to your underwear and wait for the doctor.

There comes a time when all teachers must say out loud: "If you can't beat 'em, join 'em." Your students *will* laugh at you. Might as well join the parade.

SUMMARY

"Some people create happiness wherever they go, others create it whenever they go."
- Unknown

We started our book out with a reminder to laugh and have fun at work. *There is something about the stress of education that can suck the sense of humor out of the best intentioned teachers.*

That being said, we certainly don't believe that all it takes to be a successful teacher is a great sense of humor. If all you do is make people laugh, then you are a comedian not a teacher. Instead, we ought to remind ourselves:

You work with kids, so you might as well act like one every once in a while.

You could think of it sort of like the oil in your car. It's all the other components of teaching that make the car run, but it's your sense of humor that keeps everything running smoothly—keeps everything from grinding against each other and overheating. *Humor is the friction fighting element needed for your career to make it to high mileage.* With that in mind, let's take a look at some of those other components.

Mad Skills

Chapter 2

Teaching to your personality and utilizing your unique strengths

"You know, like nunchuck skills, bowhunting skills, computer hacking skills...Girls only want boyfriends who have great skills."

- Napoleon Dynamite

It doesn't take long in life to realize that everyone is superbly unique. It may sound like an oxymoron (*you are unique, just like everyone else*), but it *is* true. No matter how many students come through our door, no two of them are the same. They have different personalities, different gifts and talents, different backgrounds, different strengths, and different weaknesses. The same could be said about teachers. *We are all different.*

Take Scotty for example. Here is how he cleans his desk: He borrows a leaf blower from the janitor and blows everything into one heaping pile. *Actually...*I think that is how Scotty *organizes* his desk (from the looks of things). He sails through school days riding on the waves of Reese's peanut butter cups and Diet Coke. For goodness sake, he even sweetens his water! His students chant cadences and every so often they can convince him to break dance (and with each passing year I think there is a little more breaking and little less dancing going on!).

Now wait just a minute! Rob has his own quirks. Many teachers work off of some type of pacing guide from week to week, but I think Rob's is down to the second. *August 23, 10:00:01 AM: Say "Good morning" to students as they walk in the door. 10:01:37 AM: Pass out Venn Diagram comparing and contrasting Colonial America. 10:02:05 AM Ask students to...* I am pretty sure he uses a card catalog to organize all his class activities, and I have never been convinced that he *actually uses* his desk because I have yet to see a stray piece of paper on it. His life outside of the classroom isn't all that different. For crying out loud, the guy has an annually appointed time to buy a new pair of shoes!

Truth be told, the two of us have *very different* personalities and teaching styles. We both have different strengths and weaknesses...and *we believe that is okay.*

One of the ironies of education is that so much time and energy goes into training teachers to recognize that every student is different. I (Scotty) should know. In high school, I was the king of different...and not in a good way! 1980's + Small town + Break dancing + Skateboarding + Hillbilly father = Odd kid. Of course it isn't just the outward appearance that makes students different. They are just as unique on the inside. They each learn differently, think differently, respond differently, etc. While we all understand this is true for students, this ideology rarely makes it to the *other side* of the desk. In other words:

Every teacher is different.

After all, weren't we all students once? So, it follows suit that every teacher, when using their own unique gifts and talents, will approach teaching differently.

Get in touch with your inner teacher

Luke Skywalker: *No. It can't be. That's not true. That's impossible!*

Darth Vader: *Search your feelings Luke...you know them to be true.*

- The Empire Strikes Back

I (Rob) had a great education professor in college who used a phrase that has stuck with me all these years. He always said: "Teach to your personality." His personality? Dry sense of humor, quirky, and an uncanny ability to make everyone in class sit just a little bit on the edge of their seat. He had a remarkable ability to "tell it like it is" yet maintain the respect of each of his students at the same time. Though he loved to flirt with the lines of political correctness, he managed to *captivate his classroom* by simply being himself.

I remember the second week of school it was pouring rain, and I had to walk all the way across campus from my dorm to class. I was eighteen and *way too cool* to carry a girly umbrella...so I put on a hat. Needless to say, I got *drenched.* I think there was a three by three inch square under my wallet that was dry, but everything else – soaking wet. When I walked into class he looked up at me, and without missing a beat said: "Nice umbrella." I laughed, he laughed, and everyone in earshot got a good kick out of it (remember learning to laugh at yourself was covered in chapter 1!). I bought an umbrella that afternoon.

Now I wouldn't recommend teasing your students the first few weeks of school, but my professor taught me one valuable lesson that semester (two if you count the umbrella). *He slowly but steadily gained the appreciation and respect of his students as he taught his class authentically.* He utilized his own personal strengths, talents, and "quirks" to make his classroom work. He wasn't the type of person to throw his arm around you, give you a cup of hot chocolate, and shower you with compliments, but you knew you could ask him tough questions and get real answers. He utilized his natural inclination towards honesty and authenticity to make a difference in his students' lives.

We believe that every teacher brings a unique strand of "DNA" into the classroom. *You have a set of skills buried deep into the fabric of your inner teacher.* What are your unique strengths? What are you exceptionally good at when it comes to teaching? Recognizing and identifying your pedagogical blueprint will help you:

Be yourself in your classroom.

You _have_ to be yourself in your classroom. If you aren't, then you are uncomfortable, your students are uncomfortable, and _you are neglecting the greatest potential you have to be a successful teacher._ We challenge you to believe the real you is something worth bringing to the table. In other words, _don't spend your career trying to become or teaching like someone you're not._

We certainly understand the pressure, but you have to believe that _you_ have authentic, personal strengths to bring to the classroom. Scotty will admit his faults, but in many ways he is that type of teacher you read about in education books. He is energetic, enthusiastic, engaging, and all around a captivating speaker with a knack for connecting his lessons to "real life." He is cut from a mold that education professors dream about. Despite his organizational skills, the man is a _great teacher_.

Even if I tried, I couldn't teach like Scotty..._because I am not Scotty_. I could beat myself up over this, but to do so would discredit by own unique gifts. I am strategic, intentional, reflective, and have a knack for figuring out the right balance between efficiency and effectiveness. I don't try to teach like Scotty, and Scotty doesn't try to teach like me. We try to be ourselves in our classrooms — to exploit our strengths.

Exploit your strengths

Every teacher has experienced the joyous process of evaluations. In it, we are exposed to our strengths and weaknesses...oops, I mean our "areas to strengthen" (don't want to hurt anyone's feelings). The natural process goes something like this: Evaluate. Recognize strengths. Recognize areas to strengthen. Create a plan to strengthen areas that need strengthening. Simple enough. (Oh, if only it *were* actually that simple!)

We have all been through this process, and we all want to get better, so what do we do? *We spend nearly all our time and energy working on strengthening our weaknesses.* It makes logical sense, but when you do so you make a crucial mistake. You unwittingly side-step your natural talents. You neglect the unique DNA *you* have to make *you* a great teacher.

The most important area for you to strengthen is your natural strengths.

It may sound redundant, but this idea is quite prevalent when you read books on business and leadership. People who achieve greatness do so by exploiting their strengths — by wringing every last drop out of their own unique talents and gifts. *This* <u>doesn't</u> *mean that you never work on your weaknesses. It simply means you spend more time and energy making the most of your natural gifts.* You find the parts of your profession where you shine brightest and try to be the *best* in those areas. I think a real world example will help clear things up.

I remember being a student sitting in math class watching Michael Jordan address the press with an important announcement. (I was in the basketball coach's classroom that period, so he conveniently decided to set aside two-step equations to do a lesson on current events!) Michael Jordan informed the world that he was retiring from basketball (the *first* time). Why did basketball's biggest legend decide to step off the court? Among other things, he said he had some other passions that he wanted to pursue. To put Michael's actions into an educational rubric:

25

Michael Jordan
Strengths: Basketball
Areas to Strengthen: Baseball

I was only a kid, and yet even I could see that there was something very wrong with this picture. Michael Jordan, arguably the greatest basketball player that has ever lived, *stopped playing the game to stand in the outfield and bat .202 on a minor league baseball team.* It didn't make any sense. It's like Paula Deen entering the X-games or Sylvester Stallone taking up ballet! But luckily for basketball fans, Michael returned to his natural strengths. *I hope the same for us teachers.*

What about weaknesses?

"Why don't I tell you what my greatest weaknesses are? I work too hard, I care too much, and sometimes I can be too invested in my job."
- Michael Scott (The Office)

With all of this being said, there is obviously a lot to gain in improving areas where you are weak. For example, I (Scotty) am a delivery kind of guy. I like to hone my lesson to make the transfer of content from me to them as dynamic as possible. By the end of a day full of what I hope to be great deliveries, my desk and classroom somewhat resemble the streets after Mardi Gras! Getting and keeping kids' attention is one of my strengths. One of my weaknesses — as Rob has so *graciously* pointed out on multiple occasions — is organization (with a healthy dose of procrastination to boot).

Rob, on the other hand, is one of those guys that teachers love to hate because he is always so ahead of the curve and systematic about getting things done. His supreme organizational skills and lack of procrastination are not natural—borderline freakish, if you ask me. In all honesty, it's a wonder someone hasn't beaten him up because of it (I know I have thought about it more than once!).

I am kidding of course. Rob will admit his faults as well, but in reality, he is a machine. I think his brain literally functions like an Excel spreadsheet. All kidding aside, I can say with confidence that without him, our 8th Grade History Department (which consists only of the two of us) would be a lot less effective to say the least.

Should I try to be more like Rob in some areas of my profession by working on organizational skills and stop procrastinating when it comes to getting things done? *Absolutely.* That being said, I still shouldn't neglect what I do best. I shouldn't stop focusing on improving the delivery of my content because that is how _I_ teach effectively. I work on my weaknesses, but try to do so in a way that doesn't neglect my natural strengths.

To wrap all of this up: I couldn't live and be happy in Rob's world, and he couldn't live and be happy in mine...and this is okay. *All teachers have their own unique personality when it comes to teaching.* Address your weaknesses but never abandon your strengths.

Teacher personalities

In all this talk of unique teacher personalities, we couldn't resist the temptation to throw in some infamous teacher stereotypes. We only *thought* it ended in high school with the jocks, the cool kids, the nerds, the skaters, and the preppies, but we all soon realize that, just like students, teachers have their own stereotypes. Stop reading right now, and I bet you can think of at least five.

As modern educators, we constantly find ourselves fighting *against* stereotypes. For goodness sakes, I (Scotty) am a history teacher that coaches—*don't you think I have a stereotype to overcome!?!* It seems that we spend all our time and energy fighting against these prejudices that we never take a moment to laugh at them. So, *all in good fun*, take a moment to read over our list of teacher stereotypes that might just be found in more than a few schools across this great nation and see if it doesn't make you smile.

MR. OLD SCHOOL. Computers? *I don't think so.* Smartboards? Last time I checked, the chalkboard couldn't talk. These guys (it's *always* a guy) carry an extra overhead projector bulb in the glove box of their car, own stock in the company that makes Visa Vis markers, and begin every conversation by stating how long they have been teaching. Purple-tinged carbon copies, hand-written notes, and still using textbooks that are three generations old, Mr. Old School is doing his part to keep "education á la 1984" alive.

MRS. CHEERLEADER. Cheerful, bubbly, and always full of energy, this teacher brings baked goods to every meeting and never met a new initiative she didn't like. She gives birthday cards to every faculty member and has more spirit than the school mascot. Her sunshiny optimism is so blinding that a few members of the staff have fantasized about making her "disappear."

THE COACH-TEACHER. Videos, videos, and more videos (VHS, of course), pretty much sums up the "coach first, teacher second" plan book. With the trusty remote in one hand and today's paper in the other, the coach-teacher gets to daydreaming about that ever-elusive state title.

MR./MRS. COOL. Usually young and trying *way too hard* to be liked by their students, these teachers dress, speak, and sometimes act like the kids themselves — more concerned with being cool than teaching content or managing their classroom. One has to wonder if they were *less than* popular growing up and are hoping the second time around they will earn an invite to the "cool table" in the cafeteria?

THE ANARCHIST. This is the classroom where anything goes (probably your favorite classroom when you were a student). Empty threats fall on deaf ears and the teacher does his or her best not to cry...*in front of the students.* These are the teachers that when you pass by their classroom during your planning period, you poke your head in the door because it sounds like the class is eating a substitute teacher alive, only to see that the teacher is in the room.

THE COLLOSUS OF COMMITTEES. These teachers burn the midnight oil. The school janitor asks *them* to lock up the school when they leave...rather than the other way around. They somehow end up on every committee and seem physically incapable of saying the word "no." Their twenty-five hour workdays single-handedly keep the local coffee shop in business.

MR./MRS. MISERY. This teacher missed the meeting that explained that a career in education would in fact involve working with children. They could start a fire with their stare and never run short on things to complain about. Negative by all accounts and perpetually miserable, they appear to hate life *almost* as much as they appear to hate kids.

THE PROFESSOR. These teachers have reached the pinnacle of teaching — in their own mind at least. The way they teach is the one and only route to pedagogical perfection. Anything you can teach, they can teach better.

THE SLACKER. Much to the amazement of their co-workers, somehow and some way, these teachers manage to stay gainfully employed. They have mastered the art of cluelessness to the point of no one ever expecting much of anything out of them. The really talented ones even manage to drum up a little sympathy in their direction for their infinite ineptness. Whether this behavior is sincere or just a huge hoax to side-step responsibility is an ongoing debate amongst the staff.

THE WORRY WART. "What if there is a tornado during a fire drill? What should we do?" Or more realistically: "Lately, I have noticed some students hanging around after the last bell. Shouldn't one of us stay late to monitor them?" It would seem that the only thing these teachers enjoy doing more than memorizing the school handbook is dreaming up countless worst-case scenarios, and more importantly, what the staff should do in response. They love questions starting with "What if…" and "What about…" and always save their best questions for the end of faculty meetings.

We're sure that you can relate to more than a few of these, and in all honesty, you probably have a little more of this list in you than you might want to admit!

Jokes aside, the thing that can be so destructive about stereotypes is that *they focus on and exaggerate the negative while totally ignoring the positive.* If a school does this, they lose every time.

A school needs a wide variety of personalities and teaching styles to be successful.

We all need each other, and we all need to be different to make a difference. When you look beyond your own classroom and unique teaching style, you will see that this is true. After all, think about the list you just read.

30

Every school _needs_...

- Some old schoolers — to provide wisdom and perspective because they have seen just about everything.
- Some cheerleaders — to keep us positive when things get tough.
- Some coaches — who always seem to be able to find a way to motivate hard to reach students.
- Some cool teachers — to connect with students in a meaningful way.
- Some committee chairs — to do all the nitty-gritty things that need to be done.
- Some professors — to keep everyone else on their "A-game."
- Some worry warts — to help prepare for what might come.

Not every stereotype is a diamond in the rough, but we hope you see the point we are trying to make: *Our differences can drive us insane at times, but it is these differences that make a school great.*

Don't believe that there is only one way to teach effectively.

Be yourself and believe that you have something unique to contribute to the school as a whole (and believe that people different from you have something to contribute as well). Students need *all* of their teacher's personalities in order to have a well-rounded education — they need men, they need women, they need young teachers, they need seasoned teachers, they need teachers teaching in the "sweet spot" of their unique combination of gifts. They also need a personality like...*yours.*

SUMMARY

"Today you are YOU, that is truer than true. There is no one alive that is Youer than You!"

- Dr. Seuss

Teach to your personality. Be yourself in your classroom by recognizing and utilizing your personal strengths. Anything less will make you and your students disinterested and uncomfortable.

Build your classroom around your natural talents.

Doing this will tap into your greatest potential to be a successful teacher, which is of course...*you. By all means you need to work on your weaknesses,* but your classroom should always be *built* on your strengths. Your gifts should be the foundation on which you build your lessons and your classroom environment. After you have established a solid foundation, then you can begin working on your weaknesses...I mean your "areas to strengthen."

Cool Teachers Don't Have Any Rules

Chapter 3

Coping with classroom management

"There are no rules here. We are trying to accomplish something."

- Thomas Edison

Ever notice how all the "cool" teachers in movies and TV shows never have any rules? Or if rules do exist, the intent is to break them. Robin Williams in *Dead Poet's Society* had his students rip out the introduction of their textbooks. Mr. Holland had his opus, and Mr. Turner of *Boy Meets World* wore jeans every day, sat on his desk, and shot from the hip every class period.

Looks great on the big screen, but have you ever tried it?!? *Of course, we all have!* Both of us tried being the cool TV teacher and got eaten alive! It didn't quite pan out like all the movies. Neither of us had students eating out of our hands, thinking outside the box, or making profound personal and academic gains. Can you imagine what a *real* school board would do if a *real* teacher actually had their students rip out the introduction of new textbooks?

In the real world (not MTV's version), teachers have rules, procedures, structure, and organization—not exactly box office smash material. It might not be as glamorous to portray efficient and effective classroom management, but it's a reality of all great teachers. Just remember: the cool teachers on television do not have any rules, but in real life the cool teachers usually end up unemployed or on the news (for all the *wrong* reasons)!

Does anyone still sell dunce caps?

Classroom management—*isn't this the reason that we all signed up to teach?* Over the years, I have been called Mr. Kuban, Mr. Q, Mr. K, Special K, Mr. Cutie, Ice Cube, Q-ball, Coach K (I don't coach), Rob, and Roberto. I have also been called an idiot, stupid, uncool, been referred to by every cuss word in the book, and even had one student tell me where he hoped I'd go when I die (and it *wasn't* heaven). I have had students hide my keyboard in the ceiling tiles, fill my classroom with one thousand origami paper boats, freshen my room up with a can of "fart spray," and figure out my cell number and call me in the middle of the night. I've got three fights under my belt (one of which was in a brand new $100,000 computer lab!) and have even had a student arrested out of my classroom. I have had my truck wrapped in saran wrap, my desks "rolled" with toilet paper provided by the janitor, and I'm sure the best is yet to come!

Luckily for the future of my career and my personal sanity, I have learned from my mistakes. While we are all tempted to fantasize about *the* job with *those* students (where everything is perfect of course), our ability to manage our current classroom will make or break us as educators. Ultimately, *effective classroom management is the foundation of our profession.* Without it, teaching simply does not exist. Sure, we all signed up to teach. We didn't sign up to be disciplinarians. If we wanted a career based on making people miserable, we would have become dentists, fitness trainers, or tax auditors (only kidding of course). Instead, we choose to be *teachers* and classroom management is a very important, *if not the most important*, part of the job.

Scotty and I are not masters of classroom management or deities of discipline (as you now well know), but over the years we have learned quite a few things that might help the newly hired and nearly retired in their attempts to wrangle untamed students.

Management myths

It's worth taking a moment to dethrone some management ideas out there that do not prevail in the everyday, American classroom.

Give them an inch, and they'll become a ruler. Everyone has experienced this type of teacher somewhere along the road. I (Rob) remember, still to this day, one of my elementary school reading teachers. In my elementary eyes, she had to be *at least* a hundred and thirty seven years old! She smoked outside the building during school, talked like she swallowed a cactus, and was the only elementary school teacher that I can remember who actually spanked students (and she seemed to enjoy it too). To put it simply, I've known snakes that were nicer. In her class, you could get a lickin' for sneezing the wrong way! What's worse, I can remember that as a "reward" for good behavior, she would play her electronic harp and sing to us. *Talk about cruel and unusual punishment!* It was like the Marlboro man trapped in a woman's body singing lullabies! Torture!

These types of teachers can range from overly ambitious type A control freaks that are strung tighter than a violin string to bonafide bullies that find a sick pleasure in their unquestioned, tyrannical rule (and some even bully fellow colleagues!). Their classrooms contain a million rules, a million consequences, and an adult that resorts to all sorts of scare tactics (humiliation, intimidation, anger, reckless confrontation, and character assassination) to make sure all the pawns stay in line.

Chances are we all had a teacher like this...*and chances are we all _hated_ that teacher*. It's a management philosophy that seems to have been around as long as the education system itself, but it's one that we don't think works with today's kids. We firmly believe you have to be consistent

37

and hold students accountable, but this method makes students uptight and anxious and leaves the teacher having to enforce a million rules. Wear your underwear one size larger and breathe a little. *It's going to be okay.*

Great lessons manage themselves. I (Rob) was taught this in my training as an educator and have to respectfully disagree...for all of us not teaching AP classes to high school seniors! After all, I have had many "great lessons" dismantled in a matter of seconds by a classroom I wasn't managing well. One lesson in particular comes to mind...

While I was student teaching, I planned out a lesson to cover the economic theories that dominated the early colonial era. I wanted to teach students that during that time in history, the world considered wealth to be fixed — one country's gain was another country's loss. I had created, *at least in my mind*, a perfect lesson plan. I held up a Hershey bar and explained it to represent the wealth of the world, and split it between students. I called these students by the names of the world's most powerful nations of the time. *So far so good* (aside from some small murmurings from students that didn't get any chocolate). I then went on to explain that a new world had been discovered, full of wealth and resources, just on the other side of the ocean. As I explained this, I pulled another Hershey bar from my bag, unwrapped it, and set it on the front table.

I turned and faced the room full of salivating teenagers and said, "New wealth is there for the taking, who is going to get it first?" I had figured things might get a *little* rowdy, but nothing prepared me for what was about to take place. It was like a T-bone steak had just been tossed to pack of hungry wolves—a slab of ribs dropped into a river full of starving piranhas! *Total chaos ensued.* Kids were pushing each other over, hitting, kicking, slapping, and clawing. Desks toppled over, and two students fell to the floor wrestling over a few morsels of chocolate that stuck to the wrapper. *It was a "great lesson" that didn't seem able to manage itself.* One busted lip and two broken chairs later, I spent the rest of the period trying to subdue the insanity and quell the rising sense of mutiny.

After all, it takes time for a new teacher to learn how to put together great lessons—what are they supposed to do with their classroom in the meantime? *A teacher that is struggling to run their room is going to ruin their room if they think that bringing some innovative ideas into instruction is going to magically turn things around.* Manage first, then improve your lessons.

Don't smile until December. We think a good teacher can manage their classroom *and smile at the same time.* This ideology does have a solid truth hiding underneath it (one we will discuss in a minute), but take a moment to think of all your favorite teachers you had growing up—did any of them wait until December to smile? Probably not. Think of it this way: *Do you honestly want to spend half of your career not smiling?*

Making management work

> *"Help, I need somebody,*
> *Help, not just anybody,*
> *Help, you know I need someone,*
> *Help!"*
> - The Beatles

It's not the same world it used to be. Most of the ways we were managed as students are taboo—if not illegal—and obsolete. For goodness sakes, a friend we teach with had a teacher that made misfits (like himself) stand in the corner while she "squished" them against the wall with her exceptionally large derriere! *Could you imagine if that happened today!?!* The kids would have it on YouTube before the bell rang, the teacher would be on the news before dinner, and the pink slip would be on her desk before she came in the following day.

Schools that use capital punishment as a form of classroom management are quickly dwindling away; however, I (Scotty) attended one where it was used on a regular basis and often on...*me!* I can remember receiving a total of *fifteen* licks from paddles throughout my career in school! I received the first in seventh grade. I couldn't imagine hitting kids in school today—most of my students are bigger than me!

The world we are teaching in is not the world we grew up in. It often feels like there is more and more "red tape" when it comes to managing students, and less and less support from home. There is no way around it—management *is* tough, but:

It's one of the most important components of your classroom.

In a sense, *the better you manage the more you get to teach* (which is what we all wanted to do in the first place). We could write an entire book on this one subject, but we're talking survival, so here are some practical principles to help you form your own classroom management strategy.

Communicate success. Don't assume your students walk into your room knowing how to behave. Show them until they are sick of it. *If you don't communicate success, expect failure.*

Be fair. Make sure your expectations for behavior are realistic. There should be enough room for everyone to breathe and be human. *If you create a million rules, guess who gets to enforce them?*

40

Be consistent. Nothing will drive your students crazy like having different rules on different days for different kids. Today, it is okay to do this—tomorrow it is not. Susie can break the rules, but Johnny can't. *Simplify your procedures enough to be able to enforce them consistently.*

Hold students accountable. They *will* break the rules...*they're kids.* Be ready to deal with it before it happens. Kids have a sixth sense to know whether or not you can handle what they throw at you. So, *who is more ready — you or them?*

Don't be their friend. This is a common mistake of new teachers. You want to be friendly and connect with students relationally, but do so with an appropriate level of distance. Why would you want to be their friend—*have you seen the way they treat their friends!?!*

Be positive. Positive reinforcement of good behavior goes a lot further than negative reinforcement of misbehavior. It makes kids (and parents) feel like you are on their side. *After all, you are on their side aren't you?*

Control your anger. Students' emotions will rarely rise more than a notch above yours. If you keep your cool, most likely they will too. Many intense situations start out as small ones escalated by the teacher's interaction with the student. I (Rob) joke with my students that: *"They don't pay me enough to get mad."*

Choose your battles. Before going to battle over misbehavior, make sure it is a battle worth fighting. Keep small things small. Sometimes you have to lose to win. *Practice selective hearing.*

It's easier to loosen up than clamp down. This is the shred of truth in the old teacher adage: "Don't smile until

December." It's a million times easier to loosen up as the school year goes on, than spend the year trying to pull in the reins after a less than successful start. *Would you rather spend the year livening things up or toning things down?*

Get help. I (Rob) was ten days into my first year teaching and ten days away from applying for a position to sell vacuums door to door when I finally asked for help. The next day a teacher two doors down the hall graciously sacrificed her planning period to watch me teach. She must have drained at least two pens onto a yellow legal pad, but she completely changed the direction my classroom was heading. *If you are struggling with classroom management, find a teacher that isn't and ask for help.*

Know when to throw in the towel. Ever tried to teach when there was a bug in the room? What about when someone is mowing the grass outside your window? The day after Halloween? Acknowledge there will be days when, for reasons totally beyond your control, your students will be bouncing off the wall. When you encounter one of those days, bury yourself in a pint of Ben and Jerry's, hit the gym hard, or indulge in one of your own personal vices. Do whatever it is that helps you close the book on a crazy day and *start tomorrow new.*

Use the sound of silence. Our natural tendency to gain control over a loud classroom is to be...*louder.* This is a common mistake. Trying to quiet them by increasing your volume creates a power struggle—your voice versus the dull roar—and usually results in your class thinking that you are only serious when you are yelling. *Don't fight for attention, learn how to command it.* A few short seconds of wait time can be the difference between keeping your students' respect and losing your temper. Know when to say nothing at all. If you aren't quite sure what we mean, ask any good mother. They have mastered "the look" that demands respect.

Don't daydream. *The only perfect students are the ones you don't have.* Stop wasting time pondering a perfect job (that doesn't really exist). It is way too easy to spend your days thinking about how well you could teach if only you had different students, but it never amounts to anything good. *Victims never taste victory.* This school year, you are where you are, teaching what you teach, so make the most of it. In other words, choose to invest in the students you have now, not the ones that are figments of your imagination.

Create your own system

"Rule #1: You will not touch anything.
Rule #2: You will not bother me while I am working.
Rule #3: You will not cry or whine or laugh or 'geegle' or
sneeze or burp or fart. No annoying sounds.
Alright?"
- Gru (Despicable Me)

"Good teachers don't need to manage their classrooms. Their students behave because they like them." *Yeah right. Convincing yourself that you are too cool or too good of a teacher to have to worry about classroom management will come to a violent end.* In other words:

Winging it works about as well in a classroom as it does in cage fighting.

When you start out teaching, *your students have a whole lot more experience misbehaving than you do correcting misbehavior!* They have spent *years* training in the art form of dismantling classrooms...and yet we remain convinced that we can waltz in the door with nothing to rely on but our own innate

43

awesomeness. If you think you can step into the octagon unprepared, you will be tapping out long before the end of round one!

If you want to survive in education, you have to use the tips we just mentioned (and any other you can gather) and create a working system to manage your room. For example, I (Scotty) use a classroom currency I like to call "Hicks Bucks." I copied a one-dollar bill onto blue paper (please don't tell the Feds), pasted pictures of my children over Mr. Washington, changed the ones to threes and embossed it with the school logo to prevent counterfeiting. The fine print states: "This note is legal tender for whatever Mr. Hicks says it is." Students get bucks to start off the beginning of the year and can earn extra bucks for good behavior, active participation, answering questions, completing extra assignments, etc. It's amazing to see the lengths students will go to earn a few extra Hicks Bucks! *Why do they care so much?*

First, if they are not failing, they can cash in their money at announced times to receive a piece of candy (amazing how powerful this is, even with older kids). But more importantly, students learn that their money is needed to pay the fines of minor offenses: chewing gum, goofing off in class, being unprepared, arriving late (I still mark them tardy), etc. It is a three dollar bill, so most of the fines are three bucks to keep things simple. Just about anything that goes against class procedures *comes at a price*...of Hicks Bucks payable on the spot. If they don't have any money, they sign my "debt book."

Once they are in debt, they have to start earning money (doing what's right) to avoid more serious consequences, very similar to...*real life*. Throughout the year, as things come up, students will try to negotiate using their accumulated savings, try to work their way out of debt, and try to stockpile their cash for what may be around the bend. I knew kids were really getting into it when I caught a couple of them trying to sell their Hicks Bucks on Ebay!

Many students ask to go the bathroom during instruction. However, when they find out that it will cost them three bucks, they are somehow miraculously cured of their need to relieve themselves! Of course I will always let a student use the bathroom, but it comes at a small price. Every now and then on Fridays, I pass out treats to everyone...everyone who is not in debt (this is when students *really* try to pay off their bills!). Occasionally, I even let students who are consistently debt free and doing well academically buy *real estate* (a.k.a. their seating location).

The concept has worked great for my classroom because it is age appropriate, rewards positive behavior immediately, creates a procedure to discipline minor and major offenses differently, and connects to real life in a way the students can understand. The icing on the cake is that the usage of credit and debt is one of my curriculum standards!

Take some time to develop your own system to hold students accountable, but make sure:

- It is *clearly communicated* and easy for them to understand.
- It is *easy for you* to implement and enforce.
- It is used *consistently*.
- It provides ways to get *out* of trouble (not just ways to get into it).

It doesn't matter what 'it' is...it just matters that it <u>works</u> for you.

Whose job is it anyway?

A question all teachers must ask themselves when it comes to classroom management is: *Who is doing all the work?* In many classrooms, teachers are working *much* harder than their students. The teacher — working their tail off — is consumed with the lesson, and the students are bored...and *bored students either fall asleep or misbehave.*

I (Rob) remember a teacher I had in high school that used to lecture every day, but a nervous tick caused her to occasionally stretch her neck and close her eyes for about a second and half while she talked. Bored out of our minds and trying to pass the time, my friends and I would stand up and sit back down when she closed her eyes. Needless to say, the trend caught on pretty quick. We actually turned it into a game and kept score!

Boredom = Bad things

Just ask an administrator how many discipline issues happen during unstructured, inactive, or idle time. When you enter into a classroom and the teacher is the only one working for long stretches of time, misbehavior is not far away. On the other hand, when a classroom has a sense of urgency, students are much more likely to focus on the task at hand.

Not to be confused with "busy work" (meaningless activities), we believe that kids should be *busy* the entire time that they are in your classroom — they should be engaged, involved, active, challenged, and responsible from start to finish. When teachers run their classroom in such a way, their students have considerably less time and energy to get in trouble.

The kids these days!

Many teachers choose to blame the difficulty they have managing their classroom on "the kids these days" (quickly citing the glaring difference between kids today and twenty years ago). For all of these educators, we need to make one final point regarding classroom management. Take a moment to think back on your childhood and recall some of the things *you* did to some of *your teachers!*

I (Rob) can remember a teacher I had who used a microphone and speaker when she taught. During class change, we would color the wire mesh on the top of the microphone with Visa Vis markers. So when she began teaching, you guessed it, she smeared marker all over her face! Red, blue, green, orange, and yellow, by the end of class it looked like a box of crayons had exploded on her face! Class was just a little more entertaining when your teacher looked like a deranged clown!

I (Scotty) had a teacher who had <u>BIG</u> hair. This lady kept the hair spray companies in business. For sport, we created little wads of paper and as she walked by our desks, we would subtly toss some of the wads into her hair (the paper landed so far from her scalp that she never felt a thing). By the end of the class period, she looked as if she had been in a violent snowstorm.

No, we are not proud of our adolescent mischief, but taking a moment to *remember ourselves as students gives us a little more patience* when dealing with kids at school. Because let's be honest—none of <u>us</u> were perfect angels either (all those kids grew up to be doctors and lawyers, not teachers). *Chances are, we all gave our own teachers a few gray hairs!* When I (Rob) think back to the time in high school when the soccer coach gave me his keys to put stuff in the locker room, and I took his sports car for a quick spin around the school...or when Scotty reflects on the time a teacher broke down and cried in the middle of a lesson because she was tired of telling him to stop disrupting, it helps us both to realize that maybe our students aren't that bad after all!

SUMMARY

Classroom management isn't fun to talk about and isn't

particularly fun to implement, but it is a *must* for any teacher who takes their career seriously.

If you can't manage your classroom, teaching isn't worth it.

Teaching is hard enough as it is. *Trying to keep your head above misbehavior day in and day out will suck every last drop out of your desire to teach in a matter of months, not years.* If you think we are exaggerating, look at the statistics for how quickly many teachers leave the profession. Focus on management until you are comfortable with the operation and flow of your classroom. Then, you can spend the remainder of your career *teaching*.

Time Bomb

Chapter 4

Controlling your time so it doesn't control you

> *"The thing all things devours:*
> *Birds, beasts, trees, flowers;*
> *Gnaws iron, bites steel;*
> *Grinds hard stones to meal;*
> *Slays king, ruins town,*
> *And beats high mountain down."*
> The answer?
> ***Time***
> *- Gollum (The Hobbit)*

At some point earlier in life, every teacher made the decision to *become* a teacher. We all had our own reasons —

BEEEEEEEEEEEEEEP! BEEEEEEEEEEEEEEEEP!
[Intercom system]
"Mr. Kuban?"
"Yes."
"Mr. Kuban???"
"YES."
"I am sorry for interrupting your class, but we are trying to find Susan Smith. Is she in there?"
"Yes, she is."
"Could you please send her to the office?"
"Yes. She is on her way."
"Thank you!"

Sorry about that. I am sure your lessons never get

interrupted. Anyway, where was I? Oh yeah... We all had various reasons to become a teacher — to make a difference, impact kids, instill passion for a content area, or have summers off (don't act like you didn't consider that!). Either way, I can assure you that *none* of the following items were on our *any* of our lists:

- Standing in the car loop...*in the heat, the cold, the rain.*
- Selling football tickets
- Pushing the latest fund raiser
- Buying items from the latest fund raiser
- Monitoring the cafeteria
- Collecting vaccination forms
- Wiping runny noses
- Making students behave
- Monitoring hallways
- Chaperoning the dance
- Calling parents
- Committees, committees, and more committees
- Squeezing into a school bus seat for field trips
- Collecting money
- Eating cafeteria food
- Breaking up fights
- Standing in the bus loop...*in the heat, the cold, the rain.*
- Monitoring assemblies
- Sweating or freezing outside during fire drills
- Working the concessions stand

As any teacher knows, there's *a lot* more things to teaching than just teaching. We're sure that right now you are thinking of a few things we forgot to add to the list above!

I (Rob) had an awesome economics teacher in high school (one of three teachers that made me want to become a teacher). Since he was so influential in my career choice, I decided to pay him a visit my senior year of college. We talked about thirty minutes and as I was leaving, I asked:

"What is the one piece of advice that you would give a new teacher?" His response [paraphrasing]:

The hardest part of being a teacher is all the things you have to do that *aren't* teaching. The secret to being happy in this profession is learning how to balance all the parts of your job that aren't standing up in front of class and leading instruction. *You figure that out, and you will make it.*

Any teacher can read his advice and relate. Day in and day out, our career feels something like this:

Grading tests + Tallying student council votes + Answering emails + Checking my mailbox + Eating lunch in twelve minutes + Completing evaluation forms + Calling a parent back + Filing yesterdays work + Making it to the bus loop for duty + Calling spouse + Passing out homework + Making copies + Taking attendance + Planning the next lesson(s) + Monitoring the hallway + Taking up a cell phone + Lining up the desks (for the 3rd time today!) + Breaking up P.D.A. in the stairwell + Filling out paperwork + Grading papers + **TEACHING CLASS**

Divided by Time
= Insanity

I think this is what my economics teacher was warning me about. *Who wouldn't drown in an equation like that?*

I'm sure we all dream about walking into school and having nothing to do but teach. After all, *isn't that exactly how most of us envisioned our career?* We imagined ourselves standing behind our podium changing the world, not sitting behind a counter selling popcorn at a basketball game! So how do we manage the responsibilities within our profession? How do we rectify our dream with reality?

Making your time count

When I (Rob) was in high school, I mowed my grandma's grass as a way to help put a little gas money in my wallet, but every time I pulled into the driveway the heat, humidity, and sweat of manual labor were the least of my concerns. You see, my grandma was born in 1918 and had no idea what that big, white square box next to the washing machine was used for—she dried her clothes on a clothes line. Somehow, in a way that still baffles my mind today, she always managed to have her *underwear* out on the line every day I was mowing.

Every time I pushed the mower into the backyard I faced a gauntlet of "delicates" hanging on the line. To make matters worse, my grandma had flowerbeds all over the backyard. If I kept my eyes on the clothes line, I obliterated her flowers. If I kept my eyes on the flowers, I had my grandmother's underwear dangling against my face! Needless to say, *a lot of flowers didn't make it!*

Why did my grandma hang clothes on a line when she had a brand new dryer in her laundry room? *Because that is what she's always done.* Americans can be quite stubborn in this regard—sticking to what we know rather than learning a new method that makes a whole lot more sense. Can you say "metric system?"

Of course, no teacher would ever do anything like that. A teacher would *never* still use a pencil grade book and a calculator to manually calculate students' grades instead of a computerized program they are required to put their grades into anyway. No, *a teacher would <u>never</u> do something inefficient or ineffective because that is how they have always done it!*

If you want to survive in this profession, you have to spend time learning how to:

Work smarter not harder.

This doesn't mean that we don't work hard (we all know we do), it simply means that we should always try to find a better and easier way to accomplish tasks. It means you value your time enough to use it in the most effective and most efficient manner. In other words, *stop hanging your underwear on the clothes line!* If you want to be the best teacher —

BEEEEEEEEEEEEEEEEP! BEEEEEEEEEEEEEEEEEP!
[Intercom system]

"Teachers, at this time please escort your students to the gym for the assembly. Make sure you stay with your class during the extent of the assembly and escort them back to class when it is over. Thank you."

"Ahhh! I totally forgot about the assembly! Okay class, nice and orderly, go on and head down to the gym. I am right behind you."

Sorry, I *completely* forgot we had an assembly today! You'll have to excuse me, but one last thing before I go: If you want to be the best teacher you can be (without forfeiting every square inch of your personal life), always be on the look out for ways to improve your instruction's effectiveness and efficiency. *You must be an old dog willing to learn new tricks.*

New tricks

As a teacher, you have a simple choice: *You can focus on quality or quantity.* Many teachers focus on quantity —

thinking *the solution* to meeting the high demands that come with teaching *is more*—more time, more work, more resources, more money, etc. This is true sometimes, but not always. We are easily deceived into thinking that more work will always lead to better results. Sometimes it does, but *just as often* it leads to burn out, bitterness, mood swings, headaches, loss of motivation...this is starting to sound like a medicine commercial...blurred vision, irregular bladder control, stiff muscles, and abdominal pain.

Typically, as our quantity increases, our quality decreases. In other words: the more we do, the less we do *well*. While we would all love to solve this problem by eliminating a vast majority of our responsibilities, we simply don't have that option (if we want to stay employed that is). Instead, we must *learn how to focus on quality above quantity*. Once you accept that you can't do it all, you are forced to start working smart, start separating tasks by importance, and start creatively getting the job done.

As teachers, we owe it to ourselves to try to get the most bang for our buck out of the things that we do. We should *spend time reflecting over what we gain from what we give*. Start asking questions like these:

- What's working?
- What's not working?
- Is there a way to do less work but get the same (or better) results?
- Is it worth my time to do this?
- Are the students *actually* benefiting from this?
- Does the benefit outweigh the cost?
- What is the best use of my time *right now*?
- What am I doing that I could cut out and not suffer any noticeable loss?

To reference our previous point, *quantity does not always equal quality*. Many teachers are working really hard on things that don't matter that much (or aren't even part of their curriculum). *Strive to be a teacher that uses every moment wisely.*

How do you *actually* do this? We've all had moments when we have been so overwhelmed that we eat lunch in our classroom (cold, because we won't waste time walking to the microwave). So there we sit with a mouth full of food, the phone to our ear (on hold with the cable company), giving a student who just walked in to ask a question the "in one moment" signal, staring at a stack of papers that we intend to somehow grade during the remaining eleven minutes of our short lunch...only to have the bell sneak up and leave us with a half-eaten sandwich, barely anything graded, a piece of lettuce stuck between our teeth, a wave of students pouring in the door, and forty seven seconds to run to the bathroom and back!

There is no doubt that teaching can sometimes feel like a three ring circus. So how do we change this? How do we make time work for us instead of against us? *How do we work smarter* without *neglecting all of the different responsibilities of our jobs?* There are no perfect answers to these questions—each teacher must find their own way that works for them—but here are a few things to point you in the right direction:

Do what is most important first. Give high priority items your best time and energy. Keep first things first. Don't give your best attention to non-essentials.

Organize your time. Assign time limits and restraints to specific tasks. This will keep one item from swallowing all your time.

Multi-task. Good teachers are pros at this. It is amazing how many things a seasoned teacher can do at one time!

Use your planning period to work. It's nice to read the paper, surf the Internet, or shoot the breeze during plan, but every minute you spend doing this is an extra minute you have to stay after school to get things done.

Don't grade everything. Figure out how to create ways for students to analyze and evaluate their own work. Use rubrics, self-assessment tools, and peer feedback activities to take a few assignments off your to-do list.

It's okay to say "no." The world will continue to spin if you decline a responsibility. Recognize when your plate is full and be confident enough to say "no" every once in a while.

Be willing to work as a team. Trust your colleagues and work together to get things done. If we share ideas, shortcuts, and responsibilities, everyone is better off because of it.

Downsize and simplify. A lot of big, elaborate projects and assignments can be downsized or simplified without losing much (if any) educational value. Ask yourself, "Is this busy work, or is it truly worthwhile to the students?"

Save your plans and activities from year to year. My (Scotty) first two years teaching, I actually started from scratch for every lesson every single day! When Joy, my wife, finally asked *"why?"*, I realized that a detailed plan book can save a great deal of time and eliminate a world of trouble.

Utilize help. Not all of us have teacher aids, student aids, or parent volunteers, but those of us who do should use them to their full potential. For those who don't, there are countless ways that your own students can knock a few items off your list (and they usually love to help).

Stop decorating, your room looks fine! Remember that you are a teacher not an interior designer. This usually applies to elementary teachers (since most high school teachers decorate their classroom once in their *career*), but some of us don't know when to quit when it comes to bulletin boards! Take pride in your room, but know when to put the stapler down.

Stop procrastinating. When a task is hanging over your head, it carries stress along with it. Sometimes we can spend more time dreading a task than it actually takes to get it done. Being proactive and getting things done makes you feel like there is less on your list...because there is less on your list!

Expect the unexpected. Teaching is full of all kinds of wonderful surprises—assemblies, fire drills, impromptu conferences, etc. Do your best to keep an organized calendar so that you are more prepared for planned events, but also be well aware that that there will be *many more* surprises that are exactly that, *surprises*. From breaking up a fight to hitting the hallways for a tornado drill to calming down a crying student to swatting a bee that flew in the window to power outages, there is no shortage of interruptions to instruction. Expect the unexpected and try to plan your lessons with enough cushion to absorb whatever—

"Will all band students please report to the gym at this time for a photo? Repeat, all band students report to the gym at this time for a photo. Thank you."

Don't forget the big picture. In all of the details, remember to keep your eyes on the forest not the trees. When you keep things in proper perspective, you are less likely to be overwhelmed.

To be honest, I (Scotty) have really struggled with this throughout my career. Time management hasn't always been one of my strong points. Like most of us in our first few years teaching, I would stay for hours after school and *still* bring work home with me on a regular basis. I was convinced that *every* student should have some sort of homework *every* night, and *every* one of those assignments had to be graded. Not only did I often use my lunch to grade papers, I even recruited my wife Joy to help in the evenings (that is when I knew she *really* loved me!). Over time, I realized that my students and myself, were working harder than the payoff. I slowly started phasing out some things, and my students still performed at the same level in class and on tests.

Some of the specific ways that we approach our classroom may be up to us (like how and what we grade), but many of the items on our list of responsibilities are not. Every educator must learn how to manage the logistics that come with the territory of teaching. This takes time, stealing good ideas from other teachers, reflecting over what we are doing and why we are doing it, a healthy amount of creativity, a dose of reality, and being willing to say "no" every now and then, but as you will see in the next chapter it is well worth the effort.

If you are in your first few years of teaching, know that it is *normal* for new teachers to wrestle their way through this rite of passage. It takes a while to develop effective instruction and efficient time management. That being said, if you have been teaching for over a decade and still find yourself over-stressed, over-worked, and late for dinner on a regular basis, you need to begin reflecting over why this is the case (and how to change). We realize that each subject and grade level has different demands, and that it can be very difficult for some teachers *not* to bring work home with them. This is perfectly fine, but every teacher should still strive to find more efficient and more effective ways to get the job done.

If you want to survive in this profession, you have to be determined to solve problems by working smarter not harder. *You figure that out, and you will make it.*

Ghost chasers

As if the latest fund-raiser, field trip form, after school meeting, and stack of papers to grade aren't enough to occupy our time, *we still have to teach!* Further still, education is a peculiar animal—one that always expects us to get better, and better, and better, and better, and better, and...you get the point. There is often an unspoken, relentless expectation to get *everything* right. We like to refer to this as *the "ghost of pedagogical perfection."* If we thought our plate was full before, the ever-present and overwhelming pressure to get "better" pulls the rug out from under us.

This added level of expectation to our already bulging list does many teachers in—their already long list either gets longer or they give up altogether. How do you survive without becoming a "teaching drop out," a zombie, or dependent on six thousand milligrams of daily caffeine intake (where your coffee thermos bears a striking resemblance to a two liter bottle!)? The way we see it, you have a simple choice.

Door # 1

Do every single thing right every single time and never make a mistake. Chase the ghost with everything you've got. If you do miss something or mess up, then do more, try harder, stay later, read more books, hold more meetings, or start a new committee to get it right the next time (repeat process as many times as needed until you are a perfect teacher).

Door # 2

Define and celebrate success. Many teachers are taught that the only definition of success is positive standardized test scores, while others aren't exactly sure what it is that they are trying to accomplish. If you don't define success, a realistic and attainable success that is, then you will never attain it. *You are trying to do everything and wondering why there is never enough time!*

Take time to define what is a "win" for your classroom.

This could be just about anything: Performance indicators, test scores, positive gains on state exams, how few students you send to the office, a survey at the end of the year, etc. Simply take time to define what exactly it is that you are aiming for in your classroom.

Success will be defined differently for every teacher, school, and system. *When you clearly define success, then you actually stand a chance to achieve it.* When you clarify measurable and realistic goals (unlike many given by the government!), you stand a much better chance of feeling like and *becoming* a successful teacher. It causes your entire perspective to shift. All of a sudden, you have a destination and can chart a course to get there. You no longer feel like you are being swallowed by a raging river of never ending responsibilities and expectations, you feel like you are going somewhere and know how to get there. *You feel like you can win, and once you win – it's worth celebrating.*

It's all too common in education that as soon as we think we are doing a good job, some new study is released about a school in Asia where students are taking calculus at age ten, and we are behind again. *It can feel like we are so busy trying to keep up with a world moving faster than us that we rarely stop to celebrate or enjoy any of our successes along the way.* This is a huge morale killer for teachers and schools alike. If we want to make it to retirement and feel like we did more than stay behind every step of the way, we have to:

Step outside of the pressure to perform perfectly and enjoy our successes as we accomplish them.

This pressure is inescapable in today's educational climate. It simply comes with the territory, but trying to improve from year to year doesn't mean we can't enjoy (and celebrate) the steps forward we take along the way.

You can choose to chase a ghost, or you can choose to chase measurable success (and celebrate when you do achieve it). It certainly sounds noble to pursue perfection, but it isn't real. It never works. *Ghost chasers don't get better, they get buried.* The teachers that make it through the wilderness are the ones with a destination, a map, and a compass.

SUMMARY

"No man goes before his time — unless the boss leaves early!"

- Groucho Marx

We don't know if anyone has ever told you this, but—

AANNNTANNT! AANNNTANNT! AANNNTANNT!
[Fire-alarm]

"Are you kidding me!?! Okay everybody, that's the fire alarm.

Everyone stay calm and quiet. Go out the door and down the stairs on the right. When you get outside, come check in with me. Stay together and NO TALKING!"

"Mr. Hicks?"

"Yes, Jennifer?"

"Can I go to the bathroom first? I really have to go."

"No! The building could be on fire! Sorry, but we've got go. Everyone out the door and down the stairs."

Gosh, it's freezing. I wish I grabbed my jacket.

Seriously? Do they have to do these in December?

Okay good, they are signaling us to go in.
Time to start heading back inside.

"Alright, thanks everyone. You did a great job. Oh my goodness, look at the time! We are going to have to bust it to finish before the bell. Is everyone back?"
"Okay, where were we?"
"Mr. Hicks?"
"Yes, Anna."
"Jennifer is not here."

Okay, I will have to deal with Jennifer later. I've got to sum this up quickly. Here are a few things about time management that you must accept if you are going survive in this profession:

- You aren't, *nor will ever be,* a perfect teacher.
- You will miss some deadlines.
- Your class will be interrupted and often at the most inopportune moments.

- You will remember as you are driving home that there was a faculty meeting after school.
- You will have some students that don't like you.
- You will forget to call a parent back.
- You will at times feel very overwhelmed by what is required of you.
- You will sleep through your alarm clock and call a co-worker to cover your class until you get there.
- You *can't* do it all.

But, you can do *some* things. Further still, you can do some things and do them with <u>excellence</u>. *You just have to choose to focus your energy on areas you want to be great and then balance all the other "have-to's" as best you can.*

If you make the right things the most important things, everything else seems to fall into place.

It is tough to juggle all the responsibilities that come with teaching...*but it is not impossible.* Good time management is a must for your personal happiness and sanity. Be willing to make adjustments and, if necessary, kick old habits to the curb. I (Rob) had a great college professor (Director of the School of Education, in fact) who always preached to us future teachers: "Don't make it harder than you have to." We owe it to ourselves to heed her advice.

You can try to get it all right—to pursue the dream of pedagogical perfection—but we will warn you: *Perfect teachers don't have a personal life!* Which is in fact, where we will turn our attention—

BEEEEEEEEEEEEEEEP!

...next.

Get a Life!

Chapter 5

Having a life outside of school

Every teacher experiences running into a current or former student at the grocery store, movie-theater, mall, or some other public location. Sometimes they are really excited to see you (and they are always the ones whose names you can't remember) and sometimes they hide (it's true), but both of us love to see the shock, awe, and wonder when they realize that their teacher *actually* goes out in public.

If you are beyond your first year of teaching, then you have witnessed this phenomenon. *It's as though students are unable to wrap their minds around the fact that teachers actually do something other than teach!* While faulty thinking plays a large part in this scenario, we think there might be a shred of truth in their confusion. The view from their desks might have led them to believe there's no way the person standing in front of them *actually* has a real life.

Don't be one of those teachers whose students aren't sure whether or not you sleep at school.

You know there are teachers like this. You probably teach with some, and who knows, maybe *you* are exactly who we are talking about!?!

What would your students say if they were asked, "What do you think Mr. _____/Mrs._____ is like outside of school?" Would your students laugh? Would they cry? Would they cuss? Would they believe that you have a life outside of school? *What would they say?* Either way, we hope to show you that *having a life outside of your lessons adds life to your lessons.*

No more Mr. and Mrs.

I (Rob) remember when I first started teaching. I kept turning around looking for my dad whenever I heard someone say "Mr. Kuban." It took a lot of getting used to, but eventually I came to be quite comfortable telling students that my first name is "Mister." In fact, now I have to intentionally remind myself (and *when appropriate*, my students) who "Rob" is:

Yes I am a teacher, but I am also a Christian who is married to a beautiful woman and am blessed with two incredible children. I am a brother, a son, and a friend. I love to write, read, run, drink coffee, eat Chinese food, be outside, and spend a little too much time watching sports...

Who are you? Take a moment to remind yourself who you are *outside* of your classroom. Why do something like this?

This profession will swallow you alive if you let it.

If all you are is "a teacher," then you may be letting a lot of people down...including yourself. Taking time to remind yourself of the other hats you wear in life will help keep balance and prevent burnout.

At first glance, it may seem like doing so takes away from our efforts as a teacher. *Nothing could be further from the truth!* We firmly believe that having a life outside of school makes you a <u>better</u> teacher.

Time well spent away from school = Time well spent in school.

70

It allows you to bring reality, relate-ability, and energy to your classroom. After all, who do you think brings more life to their classroom:

- The teacher who spent the evening goofing off with family or friends, or the teacher who was up until eleven grading papers?
- The teacher who hit the lake with friends on Labor day weekend, or the teacher who used the extra day off to map curriculum?
- The teacher who spent Saturday at the soccer field, or the teacher who spent Saturday at school?

When you value your time *away* from school (being something other than a teacher), your time *in* school is better spent: *It is more productive because you have more energy and more enjoyable because you don't feel like your job is stealing your life away from you.*

I remember coming home from work on a beautiful spring afternoon. After a snack and a little relax time, my wife, Jordan, and I took the kids to a nearby school to let them play on the playground. They had a blast, and Jordan and I lounged on a picnic table staring at the clouds. Around six o'clock we decided to head home for some dinner. As we were leaving, the door opened, and out walked a teacher towing behind her one of those rolling "teacher carts" that carries books, papers, and anything else you can dream of taking home. I thought to myself, "Sheesh. She has been at work for *over three hours* after school got out and is taking a boatload home." (If you need something *with* <u>wheels</u> to take your work home, you are taking too much!) So which teacher do you think was more likely to start the following day off on a better foot?

We hope you see the point we are trying to make here. Feel free to take stuff home, use some time off to catch up, but *do so remembering that your life needs a sense of balance for your classroom to be a success over the long-term.* Staying up late, night after night, watching old re-runs of the Cosby Show with a Cup o' Soup and a huge stack of papers to grade will demoralize your inner teacher faster than students high-tailing it out of the building on the last day of school.

There is a fine line between being dedicated and over-dead-icated.

Take time to think about which side of the line you work on.

Clocking in and clocking out

"Rest is a weapon."

- Jason Bourne

This is one of my (Rob) favorite lines from *The Bourne Ultimatum* (book, not movie). It's something Jason Bourne remembered from his training and had to keep reminding himself as he chased down his old nemesis. He understood that taking time to rest increased his mental clarity and physical stamina. Jason Bourne fighting terrorists is no different than us teachers fighting ignorance. *Okay, maybe it's a little different.* But either way, the importance of rest to my career as a teacher is a lesson I had to learn the hard way.

Two things happened my first year teaching that profoundly impacted my career as a teacher. *After learning a whole lot more from my students than they were learning from me,* it was finally fall break. We had a week off, and my wife and I decided to head to the beach for some much needed rest and relaxation.

As we finished loading up the car, I squeezed in my black briefcase above the suitcases. Jordan saw it and asked, "What is that?" I explained that I had a stack a mile high of nine week exams to grade and figured I could get them done sometime down at the beach. She rolled her eyes (rightly so), we closed the door, and headed south.

A few days later I found myself *buried* — exams spread across the dining room table — and every ounce of stress seemed to follow me to the beach. I stared out the window and caught a glance of the sun shimmering off the bay. *"What am I doing in here?!?,"* I berated myself. There I sat five hundred miles from my desk, yet I was still up to my eyeballs in work. I'm sure any teacher can relate. Luckily I came to my senses, grabbed my swimming suit, and headed to the beach.

The second thing that happened was a little less dramatic but no less important. I was working late one night when I heard a knock on my classroom door. It was the basketball coach (just finishing up practice) and heading out he saw my light still on.

"What are you doing still here?" he asked.

"Just finishing things up."

"No really, what are you doing?"

"Planning Thursday's lesson and grading papers from today."

What he said next would fundamentally alter my future as a teacher. He looked me in the eye and said: "Okay. Let me make a bet with you: I want you to put your pen down and go home *right now*. And, I bet that when you come in tomorrow morning that stack of papers will be right where you left them. If they aren't, I won't ever bother you again. But if they are, then you have to promise me you won't ever stay this late again." I agreed, and guess what? *That stack of papers was right where I left it the following morning.*

Set clear boundaries between work and life.

If not, this profession will consume you. As we stated earlier, we recognize that some subjects and grades have heavier workloads than others, but every teacher should take time to establish ground rules that will help create a healthy level of separation. These could look anything like:

- Leave by a certain time every day.
- Stay at work late enough to bring nothing home, but not too late!
- Set a time limit to what you do at home.
- Grade less (create quality assignments that the students can assess themselves).
- Learn how to unplug from school. Create some boundaries such as not checking your school email at home (*especially* on your smart phone during dinner!), or figuring out how to turn off the teaching region of your brain when you are away from school. Your friends and family will thank you!
- Learn how to plug into your friends and family when you get home. Ask about their day instead of drowning them in all the details of yours.
- If you have a commute, use the time to unwind. Whether that means windows down and stereo blaring, talk radio, or total and complete silence, find something that can help you get your mind off of school. (Word to the wise: Don't listen to talk radio if it only adds stress!)

When you do things like this, you maintain a balance that is vital to survive over the long haul. Remember, *rest is a weapon.*

If you don't set up clear boundaries, we guarantee you will eventually lose the battle against burning out.

Boundaries help prevent you from becoming bitter.

Teaching is a noble profession, but it can also be a consuming one. There is nothing wrong with your classroom invading your personal space every once in a while, but bitterness sets in when it feels like your students or school are running your life. *Set clear boundaries and honor them.* It may take a little getting used to, but we promise: *That stack of papers will be right where you left them.*

Collateral damage

I (Scotty) have read a great deal of literature about education—some that I wanted to read and some that I had to read. While I have learned a lot of great things from the numerous educational authors, I often find myself shaking my head and thinking: "I could easily become a super teacher...*if I wanted to dedicate every waking hour to my students!*" This train of thought led me to an epiphany.

The most recent book I was reading was written by one of the latest and greatest "super-teachers" (several books and movie deal). The author has some amazing accomplishments within the realm of education (and I admire him for it), but I was curious about his life *outside* of the classroom. I discovered that he doesn't appear to have much of a life outside of teaching. It would seem that education consumes his entire life.

I then started looking into another nationally famous super teacher (big book and movie deal) and found that her countless hours staying late at school led to her students' success...and her divorce. I investigated yet another prestigious teacher and found another ugly home situation. Please hear me <u>loud</u> and <u>clear</u>: *I am* <u>not</u> *suggesting that being a great teacher means you are a terrible spouse, a horrible parent, a lousy friend, or destined to be alone.* Nor am I saying that single teachers are not happy, or outstanding married teachers do not exist. Instead, I am trying to point out that: *Sometimes, the teachers that the educational realm points to as examples to follow pay a very hefty price in their personal lives.* I would even say that most of these individuals would admit to it. Teaching is *everything* to them. They should be applauded and awarded for their efforts in the classroom, but most of us can't (or don't want to) live that type of life.

Don't get me wrong: I want to be a great teacher too — *I want to be the best teacher I can be* — but I don't want to sell my soul to my classroom. I want to eat dinner with my family and take my wife out on dates. I want to coach my kid's little league team and watch my daughter's dance recitals. I want to be involved in my church and help people in need. I don't want teaching awards, test scores, and hours spent at work to be the *only* things in my life that I can point to as "great." First and foremost, I want to be considered great by the people in my life closest to me.

There are certainly teachers that live *only* to teach — sacrificing everything for their profession. I just am not one of those teachers, nor will I ever be, and I know that I am not alone. I believe that the vast majority of us want to be excellent teachers, but *also* want to be excellent in other areas of our lives as well. Finding *and protecting* that balance can be one of the most important aspects of success and longevity in our profession.

Who said I was sick?

Think this profession can't cloud our sanity when it comes to setting reasonable boundaries between work and life? Consider sick days, and more importantly, *how few teachers actually use them!* After all, have you ever noticed how teachers talk about sick days? We treat them like our net worth. Sort of like a bunch of successful entrepreneurs out on the golf course discussing investment returns, portfolio performances, and business ventures, teachers huddle around the workroom and brag about how many sick days they have built up. How many do *you* have built up? Then, every school has a Warren Buffet type (it's *always* a guy) that has been around since Columbus landed and has accumulated enough sick days to retire a few *years* early! Of course some abuse sick days every chance they get, but most teachers hate to use them.

What is it about teachers that makes us refuse to call in sick? We know: *"It's easier for me to be here, than be at home."* We've all heard it, and we've all said it, but have we *really* stopped to think about it?

- "It's easier for me to be here *(convincing myself that one more Tylenol will take care of this splitting headache)*, than be at home."
- "It's easier for me to be here *(racing to the bathroom every class change, popping yet another Imodium, and hoping my intestines don't rupture before the day is over)*, than to be at home."
- "It's easier for me to be here *(blowing my nose, sneezing, coughing up phlegm, and licking my fingers to help grab the corner of the papers I am passing out)*, than be at home."
- "It's easier for me to be here *(piling up one more day for maternity leave and praying that my water doesn't break during class)*, than be at home."

For goodness sakes:

If you are sick, stay home.

It's not a contest. *They don't pass out awards for how many days you should have stayed home but didn't.* Getting behind one day is better than being miserable for five days at school fighting off sickness (not to mention passing on whatever you have to your students!).

It's hard enough to do this job when we are healthy. So why do we attempt it when we are sick?!? *It may be difficult to admit this, but your school and your students <u>will</u> survive a temporary separation from your presence.* Get some medicine, get some rest, and give your students the occasional thrill of seeing what they can get away with when there is a substitute teacher!

SUMMARY

My (Scotty) son, Lincoln, loves just about all sports, but he *especially* loves baseball. I do everything I can to make it to all of his games, but as any teacher knows, it isn't easy. On one occasion, after staying too late after school trying to finish up grading a huge stack of papers, I blasted home and barely made it to his game. The poor little guy did terrible. He was only five years old, but he was *really* down. Desperate to cheer him up, I did what any dad looking to lift a five year old's spirit would do, and told him we would go to dinner at McDonald's! Cheap toys, greasy fries, and an ice cream cone had worked wonders in the past, but even a Happy Meal proved powerless that day.

All through dinner, my wife and I tried in vain to cheer him up. Finally, I thought of something that I believed would help. I made my hand flat and straight as if I were going to perform a karate chop and said, "Lincoln, buddy, make your hand like mine." He did so, and I continued. "This hand represents our family. This long middle finger represents Daddy, and the shorter ring finger is Mommy. The pointer finger represents you, and the little pinky finger represents Bella, your little sister. You see, we are always going to be together, standing side by side, and supporting each other no matter what. Now make a fist."

After he made a fist, I said, "Your thumb represents God. He holds all of *us* together. No matter what happens in your life, we will always be together, and we will always give each other love. You will have some bad days, but you will never have to go through them alone. That fist represents strength. We are strong little buddy. You are strong, and I promise you will get better."

I leaned back in the booth of the crowded restaurant, reflecting on what I had just said and thought, "Man, that was deep." If there had been a camera on the scene, I am sure I would have won a father of the year award and begin traveling the country as a parenting expert. *But back to reality...*

Lincoln didn't say a word. He just kept staring at his fist lost in thought. Then, he started to slowly nod his head up and down studying his fist as if in some kind of trance. A smile crept across his face when suddenly he stuck up his middle finger, pointed it straight up in the air, and said: "You're right Daddy. This is you, and I love you." With that, he stood up, fully extended his arm (and his middle finger), and began yelling out in the middle of a crowded McDonald's: "I love my Daddy! I love my Daddy!" My wife and I immediately burst out laughing, and our laughter only made him want to do it *more and yell <u>louder</u>*! I did everything I could to wrestle him back down to his seat, but he is a squirmy little booger. Needless to say, everyone in our family — *and* the restaurant — had a good laugh!

As I write this today, he still doesn't know why I laugh every time his finger singles me out of the line-up. I just smile and say, "No buddy. Remember we have to stay *together — no separating the family.*" Every now and then when I am driving down the road and someone flips me the bird for my *not so good* driving habits, I just smile and think to myself: "That's me! The number one Dad."

We should all strive to be "number one" in all areas of our lives, but no, we shouldn't judge success by how many people are giving us a one finger salute! In our classrooms, our houses, our relationships, and our community, we should try to be the best we can be. We owe it to our students, our employer, and our integrity to be dedicated teachers; however, *we also owe it to ourselves, our family, and our friends to be great outside of the classroom.* If I had put my classroom ahead of fatherhood that day, then I would have missed his baseball game. I would have missed an incredibly hilarious moment for sure, but more importantly, *I would have missed the opportunity to be there for my son when he needed me the most.* I believe it was well-worth my students getting their papers back a day later.

In your career, you have the ability to positively influence *thousands* of lives. This is a remarkable and noble calling. So noble, that *sometimes teachers neglect their own needs, work when they shouldn't, and forget about all the other places in life where they are called to make a difference.* Be the educator that you were meant to be, but never forget what matters most.

ARRIVING

Making the choice to be more than mediocre

Congratulations! You're beginning to think that the worst mistake you've made in life was getting a tattoo on Spring Break in college, not signing up to be a teacher. You've found a rhythm you can live with and can't even remember the last time you scanned the want ads. Whether you realize it or not, you are a member of an elite group that is getting smaller and smaller each year. You have found a way to be successful in a career field that sees many newcomers leave the profession.

Now you have a choice: Will you hit cruise control and coast to retirement, or will you challenge yourself to rise above mediocrity? In other words, do you have what it takes to advance from being just a teacher to being a *good* teacher? The following section will give you the tools to prevent mediocrity from taking control of your classroom and smothering your success.

They Snooze, You Lose

Chapter 6

Learning how to keep your students awake, engaged, and excited about class

"I'm tired. Let's go to school."

- Bart Simpson

"Okay, Scotty. I know you're just interning and this is your first time being in front of a class full of kids, but I think you should truly get the *full effect* of teaching. Why don't you just start out as their teacher at the beginning of the year? The class can be *completely yours*. I will just come and go. What do you think?"

I was about to begin a one year internship when my first mentor teacher approached me with what he considered to be a *great* idea. Recognizing that I didn't really have much of a choice and feeling pretty confident that I was going to change the world, I told him I would take the reins from day one. After all, *what rookie doesn't think they can handle everything?* Little did I know, I would end the semester seriously considering becoming a realtor!

"Do you know how many students will be in the class?" I asked.

"Thirty to thirty-five. It's a freshman class and kind of a dumping ground, if you know what I mean. It's not an easy class to teach, but I'm sure you can handle it. I bet you have a lot of fresh ideas from college."

There were actually thirty-six students, and my *fresh ideas* consisted mostly of mimicking my history professors and lecturing for an hour and a half. I had some great stories and good jokes so I was more than certain my

85

lectures were going to mesmerize my new students. After all, I love hearing myself speak, so why wouldn't my students?!?

It went great...*for about a week*. My mentor, intent on giving me the "full effect" of teaching, was harder to find than a class full of students who love standardized testing. By the middle of week two, the students started getting out of hand. I rolled up my sleeves and, though I didn't know it at the time, was about to begin my official initiation into education. *A scene that every teacher knows all too well...*

"Hey guys, you're starting to get a bit rowdy. Everybody turn around and quit talking! Thank you. Now as I was saying, most of the cultures in... Yes, what do you want?"

"I thought we were supposed to watch videos in here."

"We probably will at some point but not for a while." I briskly replied.

"Well, that is what my cousin told me. If we aren't going to watch videos, I am probably going to drop this class."

Before I knew how to respond, another student chimed in: "Yeah, this is *really* boring. You aren't even a real teacher anyway. Where is Mr. Montgomery?"

"I *am* a real teacher! I have a degree. Don't worry about Mr. Montgomery. Anyway, listen, don't you guys want to learn about different cultures of the world?"

With the sense of mutiny steadily rising, I began grasping for straws. I caught a glance at one of my Hispanic students and said: "José, I bet you would like to learn more about your Hispanic heritage, wouldn't you?"

"No Inglés."

"What do you mean 'no Inglés'? I heard you speaking English in the hall before class!"

"No hablo Inglés...señor."

Amidst the murmur of thirty-six students trying unsuccessfully to laugh under their breath, yet another

86

student felt the need to throw in his two cents: "Mr. Hicks, I have always wanted to ask you, why are you always wearing a tie? Nobody else wears a tie around here."

"I heard he can't even fail us," a student yelled across the room.

"Really? Well forget this, I ain't doin' nuthin'," I heard muttered from somewhere in the back.

At this moment, I began to enact almost every rookie teacher's favorite classroom management strategy — *Yelling.*

"If you want to PASS, you WILL do something! I CAN, and WILL FAIL you! And we aren't going to be watching videos for a LONG TIME. SO GET USED TO IT! I have A LOT of notes to give, so everybody PAY ATTENTION!"

"Mr. Hicks, how much of this is going to be on the test?"

"The test?! Are you serious?!? I haven't even made the test yet! All I know is that you better know all of it!"

"Meester Heeks?"

"Yes? What do you... JOSÉ! I thought you couldn't speak English?!?"

"How do you drop dis class?"

The class exploded with laughter. As I stood there, lacking the reserves to lose my temper all over again, I must have looked like a deer caught in headlights. Before my students took another swing at me, the door opened. It was my mentor teacher — carrying a video in his hand. *Never has a VHS tape ever looked so good.*

At the time, I had no idea what went wrong. I was more than certain that my lessons were phenomenal, so *how could students seem so bored and disinterested when there was such incredible teaching going on?* Now that I have been at this awhile, I can look back and laugh, and agree wholeheartedly with my students' attempt at mutiny.

Anyone? Anyone? Anyone?

You know the infamous scene. In the movie *Ferris*

Bueller's Day Off, Ben Stein plays an iconic teacher that speaks to us all:

"In 1930, the Republican controlled House of Representatives in an effort to alleviate the effects of the...anyone?.......anyone? The Great Depression. Passed the...anyone?......anyone? The Tarriff Bill. The Holly Smoot Tarriff Act which...anyone? Raised or lowered?...anyone......anyone?"

As he is lecturing, the students are staring off into space, sleeping, drooling, blowing bubbles, and obviously thinking about *anything but* his objective, Voodoo Economics. The scene resonates with all of us because, in some manner or another, we have all experienced "The Boring Teacher." From elementary to high school and beyond, we all have lived through more than one teacher's class that seemed able to reverse the earth's gravitational pull, stop time, and make class stretch unto what felt like eternity.

Unfortunately, I (Scotty) not only experienced it as a student, but also as a teacher. I hate to say it, but I became "the boring teacher" immediately. Trust me, my lessons were more effective sleep agents than Ambien! As I mentioned earlier, I started my career out pretending I was a distinguished professor of history. My idea of a great lesson involved swooning the class with my glorious intellect and brilliant lectures.

You know exactly what I am talking about. We all have had to sit through classes where the instructor lectured, and lectured, and lectured, and lectured...no interaction, no variation, no media, no creativity, nothing but Voodoo Economics for hours on end. How does this happen? How do people so passionate about a particular subject that they devote their lives to teaching it, somehow manage to bore others to tears while talking about it?

As a general rule: the more *you* love your content, the

more you think that *other people* love your content. You like whatever it is you teach so much that you dedicated your life to teaching it. Naturally, you think your content is exceptionally interesting. No need for gimmicks or gadgets, just relaying the information to fertile minds is exhilarating enough! We hate to burst bubbles, but for the sake of students everywhere we have to be honest:

Content does not equal creativity.

To put it bluntly: *No one thinks that what you teach is as interesting as you do* (except for other people that teach the same thing!). If we think students ought to fasten their seat belts because the subject matter is liable to blow them away, we need a healthy dose of reality. Students are interested in *much, much more* than the subject we teach!

To survive teaching, we must first make sure our students can survive our lessons. When students are disinterested or dislike your class *everything else is twice as hard.* They snooze, you lose. From misbehavior to low test scores to poor rapport, teachers with bored students will spend their career fighting an uphill battle. To win this battle, to make gravity work <u>for</u> us instead of against us, we have to use *creativity* to foster an interest in our *classroom and content.*

I now know that I began my career by looking in the wrong direction. *If we want to learn about creativity, we shouldn't look to experts on content. We should look to experts on creativity*, and <u>no</u> <u>one</u> is more creative than a good elementary school teacher. My wife, Joy (who at various times in her life has taught transition, first grade, fourth grade, and fifth grade), has always said that creativity in the early grades is not a choice — it is mandatory if you want to be effective *and* keep your sanity!

Creativity is simply the only successful way to manage, educate, and control an elementary classroom. Think about it. A six year old who believes in Superman and Santa

89

Claus is supposed to be interested in nouns and fractions? Seriously? Nouns can't fly or shoot infrared beams from their eyes, and fractions certainly do not leave any presents under the Christmas tree. Some eight year olds only pay attention to the lesson to give them more ideas to reenact at home when they play "school" with stuffed animals! We are exaggerating of course, but the truth is that big imaginations and short attention spans can make teaching younger kids a challenge. A good elementary teacher's classroom is bursting with creativity (an environment many middle and high school teachers could learn a lot from).

Any teacher, regardless of the age of their students or how long they have been teaching, can afford to be more creative. The bottom line is that:

If you are bored as a teacher, your students got bored a long time ago.

Trying to be creative and innovative in the classroom will help your students <u>and</u> *you* enjoy the school day far more than the apex of unoriginality—the infamous "worksheet."

Don't get us wrong, we don't think a teacher needs to re-invent the wheel each and every school year. That being said, wheels are meant to be in motion. Doing the exact same boring thing year after year will cause you and your students to stagnate, get bored, and burn out—which is far more stressful than adding some ingenuity to your lessons.

Ten tips to spice up your school life

Great teachers are almost always described as being fun and creative. Some teachers just seem to be born with the imaginative gene and others...*not so much*. What if an honest look at your classroom finds you leaning towards the "not so much" side of the fence? How do you become more creative?

There are two ways to implement new ideas into instruction. The first and *easier* strategy is to simply add little blips of creativity to spice up lessons that you are already teaching. The second strategy, requiring far more effort, is to start over (remember each new school year offers a clean slate to start something different). If you are willing to take a few trips back to the drawing board, there is a great deal you can do to create a classroom geared towards creativity.

Spicing Things Up

It doesn't take much to add a little life to your pre-existing lessons. Our first component is a prime example of just that.

1. Video clips: No, we are *not* talking about long, boring VHS documentaries made in the seventies. We are talking about entertaining, relevant, short, and fun clips that will awaken your students' minds. Google can find about 550,000,000 results in 0.22 seconds. In today's world a host of resources—*free* resources—are literally just a click away. While we grew up in a world full of paper maps, pay phones, and people who actually talked to each other in public, kids have grown up engulfed in media. They spend countless hours in front of some type of screen (instead of doing their homework, we know!). They are already programmed to receive and process information through this form of media. *Use this to your advantage.* A few minutes spent searching Google or YouTube can add just the right twist to your lesson. Most learning targets (in *all* subjects and *all* grade levels) will be better received and better retained if you can visually connect it to their brains through a video clip.

For example, to get our kids interested in our study of

Jamestown, we added a great clip from YouTube. The first colonists at Jamestown spent the early days doing just about anything to survive—eating rats, turtles, tree bark, and even chewing leather belts! To get kids hooked for this lesson, we found a video clip of Bear Grylls eating all kinds of disgusting things in the name of "survival" on his TV show *Man vs. Wild.* Teaching middle school and starting a lesson with a video clip of a guy eating bugs, scorpions, worms, caterpillars, fish eggs, and a raw zebra carcass will convince even the coolest of students that the day's lesson has some promise of being interesting.

Three minutes of Bear Grylls is a sweet trade off for thirty minutes of students thinking that history can be fun. This type of creative "spice" to our already existing lesson is a simple way to catch students' attention—a four minute scene from Monty Python opens up the Salem Witch trials, a comedian having fun with the British accent for three minutes starts the lesson on the thirteen British Colonies, a snippet from "The World's Dumbest Criminals" begins the lesson on the Bill of Rights, a speech from Braveheart fires them up before a test, and on, and on.

2. Stories: *Everyone loves a good story.* Share stories from books, newspaper articles, or even television shows to add relevance and fun to the lesson. When appropriate, and with the student's permission, you can even tell stories about current or previous students. They often love knowing that their legend lives on. But more than anything, students love to hear stories about *you.* One of the easiest ways to get their attention is by opening up and sharing the funny and inspirational moments of your life.

3. Movement: Study after study has shown that *kids learn better when they can get up and move.* We aren't talking about having kids doing a "Cross-Fit" workout sitting at their desks, but take a moment to ask yourself: "Do my students sit in their seat from the moment class starts until the moment it ends every single day?"

4. Humor: "What did the number zero say to the number eight?" "Nice belt." Cheesy we know, but kids of all ages love cheesy jokes. Any type of humor can brighten a lesson, even if they are laughing <u>at</u> you! Simple things such as adding relevant but amusing pictures to a presentation or putting a crazy question at the end of a difficult exam can bring smiles to the faces of your students. *When students are encouraged to laugh, you are creating a positive environment that will lead to better learning.*

5. Art: Most students would describe themselves as "artistically challenged" (especially as they get older), but though they rarely admit it, *kids love to draw.* Think we are kidding? Walk around and look at their papers while you are lecturing! Try to think of ways to get students to use the right side of their brain. You can do this by having students illustrate vocabulary words, learning targets, scenes from a book, or any other content related activity. Drawing requires critical thinking and forces students to visualize key concepts.

6. Music: Everyone can be moved and motivated through music. Because of this power, I (Scotty) use music in a variety of ways. Music is an easy way to get a class "pumped up," but it can be just as effective at helping a class calm down. I often use the length of a song as a timer for an activity. I also frequently play soft classical music during an exam. Sometimes I even have students write and perform their own songs! If your class needs a good wake up call, music can do the trick (instrumental versions of modern pop songs are always a hit). I try to find relevant music that connects to our learning or enhances my classroom management. Music motivates me when I am trying to get something done, so why wouldn't it work for students? Be wise about song selection, lyrics, and timing, but adding a little rhythm to your lessons is an easy way to break the boredom.

Adding a little life to your existing lessons is easy to do and can make a world of difference — a little change can go a *long* way.

Starting Over

If you are willing to spend more time re-tooling your lessons, the following tips will help build a more creative atmosphere.

7. Creating vs. Regurgitating: When it comes to covering our content, I (Rob) always try to think of ways to translate what students have to know into something they can create. This technique literally puts the thinking and learning into their own hands.

For instance, one of my standards is: "Interpret a diagram of natural resources being changed into a finished product." Now if that doesn't have fun written all over it, I don't know what does!?! For a few years, I had students "interpreting" diagram after diagram on the overhead projector. Sounds like Voodoo Economics. Then, I began having students create their own diagram. They had to think of a finished product, list ten steps to create it, then draw a diagram of its production. It was far more rigorous, engaging, and entertaining.

A lot of students picked items like a T-shirt or a pencil, but I will never forget the student who picked a "baby" as his final product. *Step 1: Cook a nice dinner. Step 2: Light candles. Step 3: Put on soft music.* I stopped him at "Step 4" when he dimmed the lights! And it would probably be best for all of us if I didn't say anything about his diagram!

Needless to say, the students in that class (and others) are much more likely to remember something they thought up and created themselves than something they learned as a passive audience member.

Ask yourself *how much of your lesson involves students as active participants or passive recipients:* Try to think of how to re-structure activities in ways that students create and accomplish rather than sit and receive. Whether it is through a class project, essay, experiment, or creation of their own assessments, give your students opportunities to produce authentic work that comes from *their* minds.

8. Groups: Sometimes group activities can feel like the six headed monster of education. While you are sure to have a handful of students who hate working in groups, they *all* need it. Learning how to successfully collaborate with other people is an essential skill that many adults today have not mastered (to put it lightly!). It takes more time and energy on the front end to manage group work well, but if you can pull it off, students will learn just as effectively (and in some ways *more* effectively) without having to listen to you ramble all period long.

9. Variety: Do you do the exact same thing for the entire class period? Do you do the exact same thing every single day? If so, *your students probably wouldn't mind a change of pace.* Of course students need routines and predictability, but some variety will help everyone (including you) maintain sanity.

10. Other teachers: Unless you are a home school teacher, *you have other teachers in your building who bring a lot of great ideas to the table when it comes to instruction.* One of the most fruitful things I (Rob) experienced my first year teaching was being forced to observe another teacher for fifteen minutes every two weeks. Get out of your room, ask around, and pick up a few ideas from some of your co-workers.

You certainly don't have to attempt to incorporate <u>all</u> of these tips into your lessons, but part of being a good teacher is being, well, a *good* teacher. Take pride in what you do and create a classroom experience that students actually enjoy. Your students don't have to like your class (or you), but everything is <u>so</u> <u>much</u> <u>easier</u> if they do. *When you look forward to your class, your students look forward to your class.* Everyone wins.

SUMMARY

"Whan Whant Whan Whant Whan..."
- Charlie Brown's Teacher

If we are honest, we will admit that there is a little of Charlie Brown's teacher in all of us—the part of our educational ego that thinks the sound of our own voice is the only thing needed for a lesson to be a success. Take a moment to think about how much "Voodoo Economics" is being delivered in your class. *If you are really brave, ask your students (but be prepared for an* <u>honest</u> *answer!).*

Bored students tend to push the buttons of boring teachers. So much so that they often push many of them right into another profession. I (Scotty) should know. I almost ended my internship applying for a realtor license.

To arrive in education, to rise above mediocrity, teachers must begin thinking outside the box to bridge the gap between students' interests and school. Tackling creativity in our classroom will challenge us and stretch us, but the rewards are worth far more than what we put into it. Do you want to be a teacher who students remember (for the *right* reasons!)? If so, give due time to constructing a more creative atmosphere. Your effort will *engage your students* at a far more meaningful level, *and help you and them* to pass

the day with much more... Anyone?　Anyone?　Anyone?
.........enjoyment.

Time Well Wasted

Chapter 7

Making part of your classroom about them

"Monday Monday, can't trust that day"
- Mamas & The Papas

G*roan.* Monday morning. *"Why* did I (Rob) stay up so late watching Sunday night football last night," I thought to myself. The kids were streaming through the hall making their way to first period, and I was mentally running through potential videos that fit our unit of study (don't judge). Then, two students came running up to me and one of them said: "Oh, Mr. Kuban! We have got the <u>best</u> weekend story! *I can't wait until seventh period!"* They ran off down the hall as quickly as they arrived. I smiled and couldn't help but find myself a little bit curious. Monday was suddenly off to a little better start.

What did they do? In a classic case of my students never ceasing to amaze me, a group of boys did something that has to be one of the funniest weekend stories I have heard over the years. A large group of thirteen and fourteen year old boys all spent the night together—a perfect prescription for trouble. As the night got later and boredom got stronger, a scheme was hatched that still lives in infamy in their neighborhood. One of the boys had a girlfriend that lived nearby. His friends decided, in typical testosterone fashion, that he needed to pay her a visit...*at 2:00 AM!* Naturally, he didn't think this was the best idea, but his friends wouldn't take "no" for an answer. So they duct-taped him to a lawn chair and "delivered" him to his

99

girlfriend's porch, rang the doorbell, and took off at top speed!

Now, I am sure that at the time, the girlfriend and the parents of all involved might not have seen the humor at two o'clock in the morning, but looking back I'm *sure* they can't help but smile. It's one of those stories that years down the road will start out: "Remember the time..."

That Monday those guys had their classmates and myself roaring with laughter as they re-enacted all the parts of their story. It took up about five minutes of class, but they helped us all forget it was Monday, forget we were at school, and forget there was work to do. Then, the rest of our class period was *far* more productive because we were all a little happier to be there.

"Wasting" to win

Weekend stories

Before going further, I (Rob) need to explain what my students meant when they said "weekend story." Many years ago, I had a lesson that turned out to be *way too short* and every trick in the book still left us with about ten minutes at the end of class—*plenty* of time for a group of thirty middle schoolers to come completely undone, band together, and burn the school down. As it became evident that I had nothing left to say about westward expansion, I sheepishly turned to my class and said, "We got a few minutes left, did anyone do anything fun this weekend?" *Crickets.* I asked again, "Come on, did anyone see a good movie, do something fun, or go on a hot date?" They laughed, and one kid spoke up, then another, and then another. Before I knew it, class was over.

The students left, and I felt good that I had yet another thing to toss into my bag of tricks. Nothing special, *or so I thought.* The next Monday, *every* class asked me if we were going to share weekend stories again. Crushed up against popular demand, I tweaked my lessons on Mondays and allowed for five minutes to share stories. It seemed like such a small thing, maybe even a waste of time, but when my students completed a survey at the end of the year weekend stories was the most popular response to the question: "What is one thing we did this year that I should keep doing next year?"

It has become a tradition that, if I am honest, I stumbled onto completely by accident. As time has gone on, however, I have come to realize why weekend stories are such a big hit with my students. *It is a structural part of my curriculum that has nothing to do with curriculum and everything to do with my students.* It's only five minutes each week, but here is what it does in my classroom. *It makes my students feel like:*

- School *can* be fun.
- Someone wants to listen to them.
- Their lives matter to me.
- *They* matter.

It's like a pyramid that builds on itself throughout the school year. Yes, most of the time it's just students trying to get a laugh (or delay the start of class). After all, I have had students share stories about:

- Castrating a bull (Remember I teach in Tennessee!)
- Falling off a dock in December
- Getting bit by a snake
- Shaving her Dad's back
- Catching the kitchen on fire
- Getting busted by the police rolling their teacher's yard (who taught just a few doors down the hall!)

If for nothing else, five minutes of weekend stories starts the week off on a lighter and brighter note than your run of the mill Monday. It also allows them to say what's on their mind so they aren't tempted to catch up with their peers while I am teaching. But as the year goes on, the pyramid grows higher. Students start to share things that are a little more significant to their life:

- Winning in sports
- Having a great piano or dance recital
- Getting a part in a play
- Visiting family
- Making a higher chair in band

Trust and significance slowly become more prevalent, and students open up about some pretty serious aspects of their life. Things like:

- Relatives sick in the hospital
- Family members being deployed
- Getting evicted from their home
- Divorce
- Death

It takes time to establish a sense of trust in a classroom where students believe their life matters, but it's well worth it.

When students feel valued for who they are, they are much more likely to bring their best into your classroom.

Weekend stories is an idea I stumbled upon by accident, but it might just be one of the most powerful instructional adjustments of my career. I would challenge you to create some type of structural component to "waste" time getting to know your students better, and letting them to get to know you (I often share a story from my weekend as well).

You will make up for the lost instructional time by leaps and bounds through the type of climate you are setting in your classroom.

Just the other day, I received a stack of thank you letters from former students (an assignment in another class for teacher appreciation week), and *almost every single student* mentioned weekend stories. *Making kids feel like they matter is one of the most significant things you can do in your classroom.*

Openers

"Okay Samantha, what do you have planned for our opener today?" I (Scotty) asked.

"Well Mr. Hicks, I actually have something to *show* to the class."

Samantha stood in front of the class and pulled out of her backpack what appeared to be a folded red flag. We all watched curiously as she began to unfold the aged and tattered flag. The class gave a collective gasp as the white and black Nazi symbol became visible.

As I watched the flag unfurl, it took me completely off guard. A part of me wanted to make her stuff it back into her bag as quickly as possible, but something deeper urged me to listen—to hear her story—so I listened. We all did. For the next few minutes Samantha told us about her grandfather who had taken this very flag from Nazi soldiers that he had killed during WWII. It wasn't a fake, and it wasn't a replica. It was a real war torn Nazi flag taken from a blood stained battlefield by a soldier fighting for freedom against one of the greatest villains history has ever known.

I got chills just thinking of the stories that flag could tell: the battles it saw, the evil it stood for, and the millions that lost their lives because of it. As I looked over the flag— every stain, hole, and tear—I wondered who may have carried it and where it had been. I thought about how the world changed forever because of *that* flag, and now a student brought it to school stuffed in her backpack like a

103

pair of gym shorts.

Like myself, the students were stunned and sat in utter silence as Samantha told the class about her grandfather. *History came alive that day.* There was no textbook, no vocabulary words, or boring time line—*World War II came to my classroom in Samantha's backpack.*

After she finished her story, I was able to lead the class in a very healthy discussion about the war and the Holocaust, and believe me, I had *every* student's undivided attention! In fact, for the rest of class, my students were silent, attentive, and seemed to act like the study of history mattered a lot more to them than it did the day before.

I believe that the beginning of a lesson can make or break your *entire* class period. The day we were all exposed to a real Nazi flag is a perfect example. Because of a very powerful start, thanks to Samantha, I had my students' attention. It didn't matter what I was going to teach that day—they were going to listen.

Without exaggeration, the first couple minutes of each class might just be the <u>most</u> important moments for students and teachers alike. This is why I like to start class with what I call an "opener." I open with a funny story, poem, news headline, song, riddle, magazine article, personal story, movie clip, "show and tell" item, picture...pretty much *anything* that will grab my students' attention. I've got an archive of openers that could be a class unto itself, and I am always searching for more because I believe that capturing your audience's attention can be the hit or miss moment of an entire lesson.

Before going further, I have to give credit where credit is due. The idea of openers is not mine. I actually stole it from a great Education professor I had in college, Dr. Ted Hipple. He always started class with something to draw us in before getting to the meat of the lesson. I can remember getting excited about his class just because of his openers. Though they were far from a conventional start to instruction, his openers connected with me as a student because I felt like his class was about something *more* than just content.

I want to make that same type of connection with my students. Some of my openers last five minutes and some last thirty seconds, but all of them are aimed at grabbing my students' attention. I often hear, "Hey Mr. Hicks, what is our opener today?" That's when I know they are hooked... when they are actually excited for my class to start.

Imagine starting class every day in a way that makes everyone in the room, including you, excited to be there.

Laughter, conviction, or inspiration—these all seem like a better beginning than: "Allison?" "Here" "Jonathan?" "Here." "Cody?" "Cody??" "CODY!" "Here." "Tavon?" "Here."

I especially like to find people doing extraordinary and inspirational things for openers. The possibilities are endless: a video clip of autistic student Jason McElwain from Rochester, NY who scored six three pointers back to back in a high school basketball game, photos of Willard Wigin's work who somehow carves sculptures inside the holes of needles, or a news report of quadriplegic Rick and his father Dick Hoyt who together have competed in over 1,000 races (marathons, duathalons, and triathlons). I hope exposing students to real stories gives them perspective and encouragement to overcome any difficulties or struggles in their own lives.

Going one step further, I try to make these stories relevant to our content: "It seems almost impossible for Team Hoyt to accomplish what they have, but today I want to talk about someone else who accomplished something seemingly impossible, a lady by the name of Harriet Tubman in something called the Underground Railroad..." These types of connections make lasting impressions in students' long-term memory. If I find something inspirational, unbelievable, or just flat out funny, then believe me, I will figure out a way to make it relevant to one of my lessons!

As shown earlier, openers also have the power to set the tone of your class. Just the right opener can silence a stampede of energetic kids coming in from the thirty minute free for all called lunch. Can't get a class to wake up in the morning? I've got a few openers that are more effective than a double shot of espresso! The right start to class can put students into the frame of mind that fits that day's lesson.

Finally, like you read at the start of this section, I am not the only one to think up the openers for my class. On Fridays, one student from each class is assigned the task. *Putting the opener in their hands allows students to be something more than a distant observer behind a desk.* It creates an avenue for them to share something important in their lives. It gives them an opportunity to perform a talent, tell about an amazing event that has occurred in their life, share some of their grandmother's famous chocolate chip cookies (along with the recipe), or explain something in which they are interested. Over the years, I have had students break-dance, sing, play every type of musical instrument you can think of, ride a unicycle, perform magic tricks, show pictures from a family vacation, pass around items they collect, perform odd yet interesting feats of flexibility, teach the class origami, recite poetry, and once even had a student perform an original stand-up comedy routine.

Why do something like this? It obviously grabs student interest, but experience has shown me a *far more motivating* reason. Just like I felt sitting in Dr. Hipple's class, students start to get the idea that their teacher actually cares about sharing a little slice of life with them and is interested in their lives as well—that they are more than a widget whose sole purpose is to sit and receive content.

For some students, this responsibility becomes a very daunting task. Speaking in front of your peers — especially as a teenager — can be frightening, but a climate of respect and encouragement is established from the very first opener. Sometimes it takes students out of their comfort zone, but challenging kids is what helps them grow personally. Often, when it is finally said and done, many want to volunteer again.

While most students handle this responsibility well, there are always a few who are, shall we say, less than successful. One in particular comes to mind...

"Okay Jimmy, today's opener is on your shoulders. What do you have for us?" I asked.

"Well Mr. Hicks, I found some jokes on the Internet that I am going to read."

When this incident occurred, I was a first year teacher and didn't think it was necessary to thoroughly review his jokes (rookie mistake). I took a quick glance, thought that they looked innocent enough, and took Jimmy at his word that they were appropriate. I would soon find out that his idea of appropriate and my idea of appropriate were *totally* different.

"Alright Jimmy, go ahead."

"My dad used to say fight fire with fire, which is probably why he got thrown out of the fire department."
Not bad...

"War doesn't determine who is right. War determines who is left."
Deep and interesting...

"If corn oil comes from corn, where does baby oil come from?"
Okay, I am not sure about that one, but the students thought it was hilarious. I will let him continue...

"If quizzes are said to be quizzical, what are tests supposed to be?"
What? I don't get it...Oh wait a minute...

"OK JIMMY! I think that is *enough* for today!"

Handing over your classroom to a student like Jimmy might be seen as a dangerous idea, but I think it is worth it. Don't get me wrong, I have had to learn the importance of pre-approval the hard way and would encourage any teacher attempting something like this to practice due diligence to make sure a student opener will be a success (appropriate for class, an idea that will work, etc.). That being said, I believe that in order to truly reach our students, we must be willing to take a few risks as educators (*controlled* risks that is).

We have to meet students where they really are, and as we all know, real life is just a little bit messy. It is not nearly as predictable, controlled, and "sterile" as we all try to make our classrooms.

Every successful teacher has become one due to calculated risks.

Stepping outside of the curriculum to get to know your students and teach them about life in unorthodox ways isn't always pretty, polished, or politically correct. But then again, *what else in life is?* The point I am trying to make here is <u>not</u> to go rock the boat, raise Cain, and get the phone in the front office ringing off the hook. Instead, I challenge you to ask yourself if the culture of your classroom feels like a place where students live out a chapter of their life learning from you, or a cold, gray, sterile hospital room where they are cured of their ignorance.

Take a few risks. Let life penetrate your curriculum every once in a while. When a student stands in front of class and speaks about her journey beating cancer or a young man shares about his brother who died a few years earlier in a terribly tragic accident, there is something *more*, something *bigger*, something <u>*much*</u> <u>*more*</u> *important* going on than curriculum. It's personal growth. It's success that will never be measured on a standardized test, report card, or teacher evaluation. It's time well wasted.

SUMMARY

Every teacher knows that gaining and maintaining student interest is an *essential* component of teaching, but from the looks of things, many of us aren't putting it into practice. If you want to be an effective teacher, do something—*anything*—to get your student's attention. It doesn't matter how you do it, but something in your classroom needs to be *one hundred and ten percent about your students*.

When you take the time to do this, it sends a clear and consistent message to your students that you *actually care about them* (and it is worth mentioning that *never* doing anything like this sends a clear message as well). It is something they will look forward to, and most importantly:

It is something that will make them feel valued in your room.

A few controlled minutes of class to connect and build relationships with your students goes a long way. Doing this well and doing it intentionally, reaps a much greater return in the other ninety eight percent of instruction. Students who feel sincerely appreciated look forward to your class, listen more attentively, and often do not want to let you down. Find ways within, and perhaps even outside of your content, to engage and maintain your students' interest. It is time well wasted. Actually, *it's time that is not wasted at all.*

" What we have here is a failure to communicate."

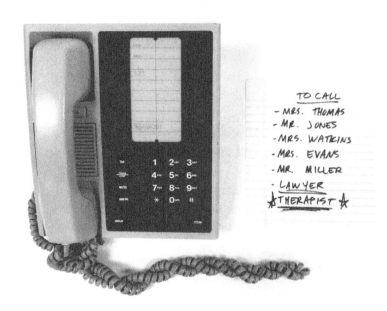

TO CALL
- MRS. THOMAS
- MR. JONES
- MRS. WATKINS
- MRS. EVANS
- MR MILLER
- LAWYER
☆THERAPIST☆

Chapter 8

Learning how to make allies
instead of enemies with parents

"You want answers?
"I want the truth."
"You can't handle the truth!"

- A Few Good Men

I (Scotty) had been teaching for about three years, and things were going relatively well. Being that I was still somewhat of a rookie, I found myself trying to work the cool teacher angle a little too much. Most teachers tend to retain a portion of their soul that refuses to grow up (why else would we have chosen to work with kids?), but I was letting that "something" get a little out of hand. I was goofing off more than I should, and my students were following suit.

Needless to say, as the year progressed, my students began pushing the line further and further until I frequently found myself getting angry to regain control. While most of the chaos could be attributed to childish immaturity and poor classroom management, I had one student who continually took things *way* too far. I had several one on one meetings with him trying to re-establish my authority but nothing seemed to work. As a young teacher, I hated the thought of having to deal with parents on discipline issues, so I put it off as long as possible. As you could imagine, things only got worse. Eventually—*enough was enough*—it was time to set up a parent conference. A week later we met. All five of his academic teachers, including myself, sat down with his parents.

His mother set the tone of the meeting by stating right off the bat that her son felt as if I picked on him during class. I defensively replied by saying, "If your son feels picked on, it is because *he* is the one that is *constantly* interrupting my class. I *have* to discipline him more." I paused for a moment, ready to bring the hammer down, ready to let justice reign, and set things right. I looked her in the eye and said: "To be honest, your son is a......*nuisance.*"

It was like a scene from an old western, when the outlaw swings open the doors of the saloon. *The whole room stood still.* A part of me was thinking that his mother was processing the various punishments her son would have to endure and piecing together just how to apologize to me for his inexcusable behavior. As the silence grew more tense, I began to realize that perhaps my accusation was not as well received as I had imagined.

To say that this kid's mom was upset would be the world's greatest understatement. *She was enraged.* I thought she was going to come across the table and claw my eyes out. If I were alone, it very well might have happened. She was furious. It didn't matter that the other teachers stated that he acted the same way in their class (though they seemed to have a much more "experienced" way to say the same thing). It didn't matter that our administrators knew his name for all of the *wrong* reasons. All that mattered was that her little baby boy—whose diapers she had changed, whose "boo boos" she had kissed, whose future largely depended on her—had just been attacked, and all she could do was defend him.

This brings me to a simple, but crucial rule.

If you make parents feel as if their cubs are under attack, prepare to meet "momma bear."

Now at the time I was not a parent, but I can tell you that if anyone — *especially a teacher* — called either of my children a *nuisance* today, my wife would be sitting in the office of the superintendent faster than you could give away free food in the faculty lounge! Of course, looking back I can see that *I deserved every bit of fury sent my direction.* I had insulted a child in front of his parents, which in all honesty, was due mostly to my inability to manage a classroom. What's worse is that I lost any hope of ever being able to manage this little "nuisance." I am sure that he was informed on the car ride home that he could do anything he wanted in my class because I was a terrible teacher, if not a terrible human being.

If you want to learn how to get parents on your side, you have to communicate. Well, let me rephrase that, you have to learn how to communicate *effectively.*

Communicate Communicate Communicate

"Hey, Smalls, you wanna s'more?"
"Some more of what?"
"No, do you wanna s'more?"
"I haven't had anything yet, so how can I have some more of nothing?"
"You're killing me Smalls!"

- The Sandlot

Many teachers would readily admit that dealing with parents is often one of the least favorite things they have to do. We just don't catch too many co-workers fighting over the telephone in the teacher workroom. While parents can be their own kind of animal at times, the years have taught us that it is well worth attempting to open a positive line of communication.

How do you do so? I (Scotty) had a former colleague who taught me a very wise proverb that I still use today. At the beginning of every year, during open house, she would say to the parents:

I won't believe everything they say about *you*, if you don't believe everything they say about *me*.

Every teacher (or parent) knows exactly what this statement means.

- "My dad said he would sign off and let me get a tattoo if I made straight 'A's'."
- "My mom always brings a McDonald's cup in with her and refills it so she doesn't have to buy a drink."
- "My dad drinks beer for breakfast."
- "My mom's boyfriend showed me how to steal songs from the Internet."
- "My dad wears panty hose sometimes because he says his thighs rub together."
- "My mom told me, 'If you got it, flaunt it.'"
- "I have a cousin that is a secret."
- "My dad makes me shave his back in the summer."
- "My mom doesn't care that I smoke."

When I think of all the *ridiculous* things students have told me about their parents, it makes me wonder what in the world they have said about me! I can only imagine what elementary teachers hear on a daily basis. Either way, it's a funny way to set up a line of communication from the get go that acknowledges that maybe—*just maybe*—there is some misinformation out there.

Addressing the need for good communication promotes a mutual commitment to keep each other in the loop. The more that you can establish a positive rapport on the front end, the better things seem to work out in the long run.

114

Don't make the common mistake of *waiting until you encounter a problem with a student before talking to his or her parents.* When you do so, you are swimming upstream.

Try to communicate positively before you are forced to communicate negatively.

Make the first contact and make it positive. Do everything you can to get parents on your side before a misbehaving son or slacking daughter is doing everything they can to turn them against you!

It really doesn't take that much to convince parents that you want the same thing they do — *the success of their child.* I (Rob) distinctly remember dropping our son Zachary off for his first day of kindergarten. We were fortunate enough for my wife Jordan to be a stay at home mom, so dropping him off at school was a *big* deal for Zachary...*and especially Jordan!* (I'd be lying if I acted like I didn't shed a few tears myself.) After a few half days and many tears, Jordan was still skeptical about entrusting her son to a total stranger. Zachary's teacher seemed nice, Zachary really liked her, and everything looked great on paper, but momma bear still wasn't quite sure about letting one of her cubs out of her sight. *Then something strange happened.*

Out of the blue, Zachary's teacher called home to tell Jordan that he was doing great, he was adjusting well, and she thought he was a well-behaved, sweet, sincere, and smart young boy. That call was a bigger hit than Joe Carter's home run to win the 1993 World Series. Jordan may have started out a little bit skeptical, but after three minutes of unexpected phone time she probably would have taken a bullet for Zachary's teacher! Not surprisingly, my son's kindergarten teacher proved to be an incredibly talented and caring teacher.

A little goes a long way with a parent.

Do something—*anything*—to start creating positive relationships with your students' parents. Even the smallest gesture can make a lasting impression.

One of the most powerful things a teacher can do is personally reach out to a parent—by telephone, a handwritten note, or even an email...*with nothing but good things to say.* When I first started teaching and had no clue how to manage a classroom, I found that if I called home (on a good day) and sung their child's praises (for *that* day at least), I left many parents speechless. I have literally had parents tell me: "I don't know what to say. I have never had a teacher call and tell me something good." Much like my son's kindergarten teacher, if you can catch a student doing something good—and let mom, dad, grandma, and whoever else know about it—then you have a parent on your side for life. Not to mention, in many cases, the student as well.

The number one thing a parent wants to know is that you <u>care</u> about their child.

That's it. If parents think you care about their kid, they usually think you are a good teacher. If parents think you *don't* care about their kid, they usually think you are a bad teacher. This may be a tad over-simplified way of looking at it, but the point remains the same. *A parent's perception of whether or not you genuinely care about their child often determines if they are standing in your corner or strapping on gloves from the other side of the ring.* You can have all the academic credentials in the world, but those credentials don't mean a thing to a parent who thinks you don't care. *Win this battle.* Show parents that you <u>do</u> care...because you do.

Allies or enemies?

When it comes to parents, you are dealing with a very powerful asset—one that is either working for you or against you. *Great teachers will do what they can to pull that influence in their favor.* You have nothing to lose and everything to gain by creating assets instead of adversaries when dealing with parents.

We have met with hundreds of parents over the years. Although they vary in personalities, child-rearing philosophies, discipline structures, expectations, and sanity, they all seem to have one thing in common:

All parents want their children to be successful.

Even terrible parents, and every teacher has certainly met their fair share of them, *want* their children to succeed. They may not be willing to put forth any effort or enforce any consequences to steer their kids toward success, but *the desire to see their child do well exists in every parent.*

It is essential that you form alliances with parents. To do so, you have to *capitalize on every parent's desire for their child's success.* Try to convey to parents that everything you do in your classroom is done in an honest effort to help their child be successful. If you can convince them of this, then their power of influence is on your side. In other words, it's in your best interest to keep a student's best interest in mind. It creates a win-win situation. You are happy, the parents are happy, and (though it may not make them happy at the time!) students are steered towards success.

No one benefits when parents become adversaries.

Parents can be extremely trying at times, but it simply

117

isn't worth the temporary trumpeting of our ego to make enemies with a parent. A parent that is against you has virtually unlimited potential to protest your continuance in the profession (and these parents *always* seem to have virtually unlimited amounts of free time as well!). To state it bluntly, parents can pretty much say just about anything to a teacher, but we risk our jobs and reputation if we don't keep our cool. Is that fair? Of course not. But, unfortunately, *it is what it is.* In light of this, a wise teacher will realize that nothing good can come of making enemies with parents and will thereby make every effort to keep a parent in the "ally" category.

You will certainly encounter a few parents who won't be happy regardless of what you do — often repeat offenders who think complaining should be an Olympic sport — and chances are your administration knew them long before they called to complain about you! But *even in these situations you need to be diplomatic and professional.* You can't control their actions, but you can always control yours.

Who you calling crazy?

It's easy to make allies with rational, stable, emotionally-balanced, and well-mannered adults. *No need for advice when you have Mayberry on the other end of the line* (as if you actually have to call those kids' parents anyway!). Unfortunately, as we all know, there are plenty of parents that would be more closely associated to Otis than to Sheriff Taylor. How do you handle an adverse parent interaction?

1. Remain calm and professional. Never get angry. *You can't accomplish anything positive with a parent when you are angry.* You will say things you will regret and, like the story at the beginning of this chapter, any hope for improvement will go down the drain.

2. Let them voice their concern *first*. This is especially true if they called you. *They didn't call you to listen.* They want to talk. They won't listen to anything you say until you let them say their peace.

3. Before *anything* negative comes out of your mouth, say something positive. When you start out the conversation saying that you like having their son or daughter in class, or that you appreciate their kid's sense of humor, or that you see great potential in their child, *their defenses will come down.* You have to convince them that you are on their kid's side for any good to come of the conversation.

4. Clear up any misinformation. Often we are talking to parents about a situation in which their only source of information is their child. Often, *things are just misunderstood, misheard, or miscommunicated* and a solution involves nothing more than getting everyone on the same page.

5. Be realistic and look for a solution with *their input*. *Asking parents what they think should be done* to fix things ensures that they feel like they have been heard and they have a voice in their child's education. It also makes parents believe that you want their child to be successful.

6. Document *everything*. In today's world, *it is worth making note of conversations with parents.* This gives you and your administration more freedom (and protection) moving forward.

7. Contact guidance and request not to have any younger siblings. Kidding, *only kidding*...sort of.

When I (Scotty) was thinking about a real conversation I have had with a parent that could illustrate these principles, one rather memorable conversation came to mind. It occurred during one of my most "uncomfortable" times in life. I missed school for a doctor's appointment, and it happened to be a day when my students were taking an exam. One of my students was absent the day prior and missed our review session. The substitute was unaware of this student's absence and made her take the test anyway. She bombed it, and a few days later I was on the phone talking to her mother.

"Hello, this is Mr. Hicks from the middle school. I was told you needed to speak with me." *(Stay calm and let her talk first.)*

"You are absolutely *right*. I *do* need to speak with you. You made my daughter take an exam that she was *not* prepared for. She told me that she wasn't even given the study guide that *every* other child received. Do you do that every time a student of yours is absent Mr. Hicks? Because I can tell you it is not fair. She did *not* deserve a failing grade. She has been upset all weekend. You do realize that school policy states she does not have to take an exam immediately after being absent. She was throwing up all night! Would you have liked me to have sent her to school sick so she could have thrown up everywhere? Plus...."

All I could do was just sit and listen, which I did for quite a while. I envisioned her twirling her head and snapping her fingers in the air from side to side as she spoke. She was obviously very upset and had *a lot* to get off of her chest. When she finally stopped to take a breath, I made my move. *(Say something positive and clear up misinformation)*: "I am glad to hear that your daughter is feeling better now. I am extremely sorry for the misunderstanding. I was also surprised to see that grade as well. She is a very studious young lady who rarely makes anything below an "A". I had a substitute teacher that day and he was unaware that she was absent." I continued to tell her the whole situation was due to miscommunication on several levels. *(Let her help figure out a solution.)* I then asked her, "What do you think would be the fair thing to do about the exam under the circumstances?"

"Well I think she should be able to re-take the test," she said.

"As do I. I will give her another version of the test as soon as possible. Is there anything else you are concerned about?"

The situation was diffused, a reasonable solution was set, and now it was time to exit stage left as quickly as I could. To be honest, I think she was a little disappointed that it was resolved so quickly and there was nothing else to argue about.

"Well I just want to know why you didn't tell the substitute she was absent? That test has dropped her grade one full letter. It doesn't matter that she gets to re-take the test. Her spirit is crushed. She has never..."

At this point I realized that there wasn't anything else I could do to make things right in her eyes. I did my best to stay calm and professional, and tried to end the conversation: "If that is all you are concerned about, again I am sorry about the miscommunication, but I need to get off the phone and start putting together that re-test..."

"Mr. Hicks, *have you not heard what I am telling you?!?* My daughter is extremely upset. You need to make sure this kind of thing never happens again. I think you may have been absent during another exam earlier in the year. Do you try and miss all exam days? What were you doing missing school on an exam day anyway?"

Now she was getting personal. Though she seemed to think otherwise, it was none of her business what I was doing that day. I had tried to diplomatically end the conversation twice, but she would not be satisfied with much less than my official resignation from the profession. As I saw it, I was left with three options: get angry and fight fire with fire, hang up, or tell her the truth about where I was that day. I chose the latter.

"Well, if you really want to know, I missed school because I had a vasectomy. I found it extremely difficult to walk because of the severe pain and swelling in my groin. So due to that and my doctor's recommendation, I decided to take it easy for a few days."

Very long silence...

"Hello?" I asked into a phone line that appeared to have just gone dead. I waited a few more moments and then uttered again into the void, "Hello? Are you still there?"

"Oh... Okay... Well thanks for taking care of the problem. Good bye."

She never called again.

Now that I am dealing with teachers as a parent, I am a little more sympathetic to the parents who sit on the other side of my desk—even the ones I have poked a little fun at in this chapter. *Being a parent makes you realize that parents aren't quite as crazy as you used to think!* Even difficult parents are usually just trying to do what they think is best for their child. The view from their side of the desk is completely different. All parents can get a little crazy when it comes to their children. Remembering that will help you keep things in perspective, seek their input, and be grateful that you will only be dealing with their child until summer vacation...not the rest of your life!

Apples falling too close to the tree?

How often have you scheduled a meeting to address tardiness only to wait ten minutes for the parent to arrive? How about a meeting pertaining to absences and the parent is a no-show? Ever have a student who consistently loses focus in class, and a parent conference results in a screaming match between his mom and dad? What about dress code? Ever scheduled a meeting with Mom because her daughter isn't following dress code and Mom walks in looking like she, well, let's just say she isn't following dress code either!

As the old saying goes, "The apple doesn't fall far from the tree." What do you do when *the problem* with your students is that *they fell too close to the tree?* From bad attitudes to bad work habits to bad manners, every school in America has difficult students and hiding behind these kids are often parents feeding (or enabling) their misbehavior.

What do you do when you feel like making an ally with a parent would be about as useful as an alliance with Antarctica in World War Three? What about the mom, dad, grandmother, or grandfather in charge of the child who seem all but invisible? Maybe the parents (or parent) are not involved because they are working like crazy just to keep food on the table and the lights on. Or maybe the family is wealthy, but mom and dad are too busy making money to be parents. Perhaps the message of this chapter doesn't seem like it works for your classroom or school community. *What then?*

I (Rob) started my career teaching eighth grade in an urban school. If I remember correctly, the eighth graders I taught would feed into what the first No Child Left Behind report ranked as the third worst performing high school in the forty seventh worst performing state. Needless to say, there wasn't a long line at the P.T.A. table! I met with several parents who didn't make it past the eighth grade. I had students with parents in jail. I had four students that were already parents themselves. Once I even had to lock a student in my classroom because his father (without any custody rights) was circling the school with a shotgun demanding to see his son.

In my experiences from urban to suburban schools, I found that: *Every parent really does desire their child to be successful, and nearly every parent brings something to the table.* Meeting with parents at my first school had plenty of advantages. They *never* thought their child was an angel, and they *always* trusted my authority and competence as a teacher (a couple areas where teachers in suburban schools may have a little more difficulty). Even when you think a parent has nothing to bring to the table, risk believing that they do...and you might just find yourself pleasantly surprised.

There are certainly times when a call or email amounts to nothing, but there will be just as many, if not more, occasions where dramatic changes occur after mom or dad covers the receiver and starts screaming all three birth names into the living room! I (Scotty) once taught a young lady who constantly wanted to visit the school nurse, but seemed especially under the weather when we were taking a test or working on an assignment. After multiple visits when the nurse diagnosed her with an "allergy to work," I set up a conference with the mother (to see if perhaps there was a deeper cause for the problem). After exposing the truth, this girl's mother gave her daughter a good ol' fashioned hickory stick verbal whipping right in front of her teachers! I will never forget the mother's words:

"Mr. Hicks, she would call me every time she visited the nurse. After the first few times, I actually came and picked her up. But then I started to realize it was all a front for *laziness*. I do not tolerate laziness Mr. Hicks. The next time she called, I told her to get her %$* back to class! You know what she tried to tell me? 'Mom, you can't say that! They might be recording this!' I told her: Good! Then, they can play it back to you every time you ask to visit the nurse!"

Dealing with some parents can be tricky to say the least, but every parent has a right to know what is going on with their child (just think of your own children in school). Even if we have a suspicion the parent is part of the problem, we have to communicate and give parents the opportunity to do what they should. This process can be uncomfortable and awkward (like the situation above), but once again we will often find ourselves surprised with how fruitful reaching out to a parent can be.

124

Finally, the honest truth is that not all parents out there will make a positive difference in their child's life. Every teacher has run into parents that are, to put it politely, rather useless and even counterproductive when it comes to guiding their child towards success. In fact, some parents even seem as if they are trying to push their children towards failure. Taking the time to connect with a parent (if opportunity allows) may give insight into your student's life that you otherwise wouldn't know. Unfortunately, many students are troublesome because they are living in a troublesome home.

Teachers are the <u>only</u> positive role models in many kids' lives.

Do not take this lightly. Troubled, difficult students *need* a teacher like you to show them how to uproot and plant their tree a little farther from where their apple fell (a later chapter will look specifically at how to work with these kids). You have the opportunity to redirect their lives, and who knows, maybe their parents will take the cue and start acting like...parents.

SUMMARY

We have seen a variety of parents and parenting skills (and there are sure to be *plenty* of <u>new</u> adventures lying right around the bend). Here are some classics:

- A mother who slapped her six foot one, fifteen-year-old son across the face during a conference.
- A set of parents who explained that their experience teaching Sunday School gave them just as much insight into education as any teacher.
- A father who tried to convince me that I was

changing American history and not teaching it correctly.

- A set of parents who stated it was their personal parenting philosophy to never make their son do anything he didn't want to do.
- A mother who wrote a letter to the superintendent because I required my students to read novels in order to gain admittance to Honors classes.
- A mother who was in shock that her son got angry when she told him that the man he grew up thinking was his dad really wasn't his father.
- A father who stated that the track workouts were inadequate for his "thirteen year old collegiate level athlete."
- A mother who told me that my expectations for her son were too high, and I needed to "chill out."

While these kinds of parents inspire the best stories in the faculty lounge, the reality is that the average parent is *far* from the list above. In fact, there are just as many, if not more, outstanding parents. Over the years, we have seen plenty of these as these as well.

- A working single mother raising three boys who refused to miss an open house or allow her boys make any grade below a "C."
- A set of parents with *eight* kids that could easily be the poster children for manners.
- A father who required his daughter to read four additional content relevant novels per grading period.
- A set of parents who took their children to Colonial Williamsburg because of what they were learning in class.
- A set of grandparents who poured their heart and soul into the upbringing of their granddaughter

whose mother was addicted to drugs.

- A set of parents who paid for their own child to go on an eighty dollar field trip, as well the costs for five other children who wouldn't have otherwise been able to go.
- Parents who volunteer so often that most of the staff think they are part of the faculty.
- Moms and dads who sit in the stands to support their child at every single game.
- Parents who hug and kiss their child, and tell them they love them (even when they are grown up) *every day* before school.

If we let the occasional, let's just say "unfortunately memorable," parent to be an excuse to write off all parents, then we have made a grave mistake. *We must not allow a few discouraging parents to deter us from the many well meaning, invested, and loving ones.* Most mothers and fathers love their children *very much* and are willing to do whatever they can in the name of their child's well being—academically and otherwise. Respect that devotion, honor that commitment, and *use* that love to mold the sons and daughters in your class. We owe it to our students to do what we can to befriend their (and our) number one ally—*Parents.*

" I fought the law, and the law won."

REVISED
STATE
STANDARDS

Chapter 9

Surviving the latest trends and the evaluation process

"They say that nobody is perfect. Then they tell you practice makes perfect. I wish they'd make up their minds."

- Winston Churchill

Fads. From popping slap bracelets to popping collars, from Chuck Taylors to Crocs, from teasing hair to greasy hair to Justin Bieber's hair, from baggy jeans to skinny jeans to tight rolling jeans to cutting jeans to sagging jeans to ripping jeans to "Daisy Duking" jeans...the latest craze is coming to a classroom near you. However, any seasoned educator can tell you that fads are *certainly not limited to students!* Anything below look familiar?

Word Walls	*Think, Pair, Share*
Pre-Tests	*Hands-On Teaching*
P.A.R.S.	*Common Core*
Bulletin Boards	*Standards-Based Grading*
Power Teaching	*Differentiated Instruction*
No Child Left Behind	*Test Re-takes*
Best Practices	*Researched-Based Strategies*
Career Education	*Multiple Learning Styles*
Ability Grouping	*Writing Across the Curriculum*
Time for Time	*Reading Across the Curriculum*
Cooperative Learning	*Interdisciplinary Projects*
Manipulatives	*Rubric-Based Assessments*
Cornell Notes	*Left Brain vs. Right Brain*

Graphic Organizers	Costa's Levels of Questioning
Marzano's Nine	Literacy for All Learners
Critical Thinking Skills	Integrated Curriculum
Team Teaching	Multicultural Education
Focus Groups	Multiple Intelligences
Learning Targets	Student-Friendly Terms
Visual Learning	Critical Friends Groups
Auditory Learning	Bubble Kids
Kinesthetic Learning	Technical Reading
Tracking	Inquiry-Based Teaching
Vertical Alignment	Learning Centers
Horizontal Alignment	Flipping the classroom
Bloom's Taxonomy	Constructed Response
Current Events	Character Education
Looping	Guided Reading
Phonics	Whole Language

As you are well aware, we could go on, and on, *and on* (and you could certainly add a few <u>more</u> yourself!). What do all these things have in common? At one point, they were the latest and greatest, once and for all, solution to successful teaching.

We don't mean to sound cynical—*we believe that every item on this list can be a valuable tool in today's classrooms.* The concern is that many teachers feel the need to implement *every item on the list!* It's sort of like using a salad plate at the all-you-can-eat buffet. Everything looks great, but you only have room for so much (and many of us have eyes that are bigger than our stomachs). After all, when these ideas were first introduced at a faculty meeting, in-service session, or professional development seminar they were more than likely presented as the strategy that would move students to the next level. And just like that, another item or initiative is added to our "to do" list. Then, a year or two later, when another strategy gets introduced as the new primary focus, teachers are rarely told to *stop* doing the previous strategy. To put it simply, *there is much more being added to our plates than removed* (not to mention that us teachers can be quite stubborn when it comes to letting go of our own classroom traditions). This process can be overwhelming at times — especially to new teachers — and just to make it *even more* interesting, we refer to most of these strategies and initiatives using acronyms!

So how do you keep from getting motion sickness when your classroom is tossed about on the waves of change year after year? It may be simpler than you think.

Surviving the trends

"Come gather round people wherever you roam
And admit that the waters around you have grown
And accept it that soon you will be drenched to the bone
If your time to you time is worth saving —
You'd better start swimming or you'll sink like a stone
For the times, they are a changing."
- Bob Dylan

The times, they <u>are</u> a changing. Sometimes we wonder if Bob Dylan was a teacher. After all, doesn't admitting the waters have rose, getting drenched to the bone, and learning to swim so you don't sink like a stone sound a little like education? The constant state of change, and even more so, the necessity to adapt to those changes is a crucial survival skill for every educator.

When we set out to write a book that would help teachers make the most of their classroom, we did what any good authors would do — consult with the experts. First stop: the politicians who have been making all of these new improvements to education over the last several years. Quickly, we realized that most of them have *never taught a day in their lives* and thereby would not be a very good source of advice for teachers. Next, we turned our focus towards some of the distinguished educational "super-

131

professionals." These are the powerhouses who publish article after article, conduct massive research projects, and serve on government committees. Regrettably, they were all too busy *outside of a classroom* — writing more articles, crunching data, inventing new theories, or lecturing about how lecturing is not effective — to help those of us *inside of a classroom.*

We hope you see that we are being a little facetious here — venting some steam perhaps? After all, we recognize that there are many educational leaders and politicians genuinely striving to make a positive and meaningful impact on America's educational system. Despite the hints of sarcasm, the point remains the same. One of the most frustrating realities of education today is: *It can feel like the more important the decision is, the further from your classroom is the person making it.*

We know how exasperating it can be when some new policy, law, or procedure affects your classroom, *especially* when your plate is already overflowing. The resulting stress causes many educators to yearn for retirement. You can get angry and pout, or muster whatever energy you have left to resist change, but you are fighting a lost cause. Think about it this way:

- *Which politician is going to get elected?* The one who will keep schools the same, or the one who will make drastic improvements?

- *Which professor is going to get published?* The one teaching established methods, or the one doing new, revolutionary research that will change the face of education?

- *Which educational research firm is going to get a grant?* The one studying timeless truths, or the one analyzing the latest breakthrough that will launch American education to the next level?

The very foundations of our educational leadership structure demand a continuous push forward to "the next big thing." To put it plainly, it's a competition. *Those responsible for many of the changes in education have to keep evolving, or they will be the ones left behind.* Trends aren't going anywhere. They will continue for eternity, but consider the alternative: A constant state of complacency where we no longer care if our students, our schools, or our country are improving.

The powers that be, the ones who ultimately steer the ship of American education, are forced by the nature of their position to be *idealistic*. You, on the other hand, are forced by the nature of your position to be *realistic*. It only makes sense that these two worlds won't always connect. *Teaching at the intersection of rhetoric and reality isn't always easy, but it isn't impossible either.* In the grand scheme of things, the best choice for your future stability (and sanity) is to:

Surrender to the fact that education is always going to be changing, and admit that change can be good.

"If your time to you is worth saving," as Mr. Dylan so aptly wrote, then the first step is to accept these truths. It can be a bitter pill to swallow (especially for younger teachers), but a tangible peace follows after admitting to yourself that — *unfortunately* — the educational system in America is *not* going to conform to your personal teaching philosophy.

Once you have surrendered to this reality, there are a couple things you can do to survive the trends without becoming cynical. Here are some suggestions:

Be willing to learn. American culture, parental expectations, collegiate requirements, and society in general are constantly changing. When I (Rob) was a kid, I had to show my parents my *completed* homework before I was allowed to play Super Mario Brothers. Even then, I had a strictly enforced thirty minute time limit before I had to turn the Nintendo off. Nowadays, I have parents that allow their children to miss a day of school because a popular new video game was released at midnight the night before.

Since you live in a culture that is constantly changing, do you really think that you can be a successful teacher year after year if your strategies don't change? If the world is moving and your classroom isn't, sooner or later the two won't be able to connect.

Start off by recognizing that there is something good in every trend. The best teachers will always try to improve instruction and let new ideas be part of shaping their classroom. If you embrace this outlook, then you go into a professional development session a little more optimistic — a little more willing to believe that you might learn something that will help you improve as a teacher. This doesn't mean re-inventing your classroom around every trend, it simply means that your instructional practices are evolving with the world in which you are teaching.

Be willing to wait. Fads, by definition, are fleeting. When I (Rob) was being trained as an educator, the word "textbook" was taboo. I was more or less taught that teachers who regularly use the textbook are uncreative, ineffective, unprepared, lazy, and boring. I even remember one professional development session when the guest speaker called textbooks "training wheels" for new teachers. What point am I trying to make here? Just the other day, I attended a professional development session hosted by one of the industry's most cutting edge research organizations. Their findings? The biggest gap between American schools and other advancing countries is technical reading skills. Their solution? Students need to spend more time reading, that's right, *their textbooks.*

If you aren't the biggest fan of the latest trend, don't

worry it will change with the next election cycle, policy shift, best-selling book, school board, or educational summit.

Make trends fit your classroom rather than making your classroom fit trends.

If you teach well, there is no need to re-invent your classroom with each passing fad. You will drive yourself and your students crazy. Instead, focus on teaching effectively and use the latest ideas to fine tune your lessons. *If you try to do everything, you will do nothing well.* Teach well, be willing to wait, and you will make it. As the old teacher saying goes, "This too shall pass."

While it may sound like a contradiction, surviving the barrage of change involves being willing to learn <u>and</u> being willing to wait. Picture a suspension scale balancing two weights. If you try to change with every fad, you will go crazy. On the other hand, if you try to hold on to the way you taught twenty years ago, your students (and administration) will go crazy. Strive for a balance that works for you, your students, *and* your administration.

Rolling with the punches

"Serenity now!"
> - Mr. Costanza (Seinfeld)

After you have been teaching a while, you begin to realize just how much (and how fast) education changes, and more importantly, how that affects *you*. For example, it took us just under a year to write this book. During that short span of time we have had to:

- Move classrooms as part of a system-wide

135

reorganization of students, teachers, and facilities.
- Build relationships with dozens of new staff members (almost *half* of our staff was new to the school building).
- Re-structure our lessons because we shifted from a forty-four minute period to a seventy-four minute period.
- Re-configure our instruction because the new schedule put our subject and students on an A/B rotation.
- Learn the ins and outs of our state's new evaluation model.
- Adjust to a new operating system on our computers.
- Figure out how to use the new school website.
- Adapt our instruction to the new points of emphasis from our state and our system.
- Take nearly everything back out of our classrooms so that a new HVAC unit can be installed over the summer.

Sound like a lot? We saved the best for last: Halfway through the school year, we received an email from the state informing us that they are completely re-distributing the curriculum for Social Studies in grades 6-12. The subject we teach may no longer be part of the 8th grade curriculum (unless they change their mind, of course!). We are either moving to another grade or will be teaching an entirely new curriculum in the not too distant future. As we write this, we aren't even sure what we will be teaching next year!

This amount of change in less than a year sounds crazy to anyone...*who isn't a teacher.* We are so used to things changing that we almost get a little surprised when something stays the same. The constant state of change creates a variety of responses from teachers. Some get *stressed:* How can we do this? When is there time? Some get on a *soapbox:* Why do we have to do this? Why can't I teach the way I want to teach? Some simply *give up*: Anyone know of an open sales position? The teachers who make it, without getting ulcers, are the ones that utilize a different strategy — they roll with the punches.

There comes a time when every teacher must choose to roll with the punches or take a beating. Change will *always* be part of education. Do your best to utilize the strategies laid out in this chapter to survive the latest trends, but also realize that there is a part of you that is going to have to learn how to let things roll off your back without ruffling your feathers. Speaking of taking a beating...let's move on to evaluations!

Evaluations

Evaluations. Oh, the humanity. I (Scotty) will never forget my very first evaluation. It was a train wreck to say the least. From the moment it was scheduled, I began preparing what I thought would be a phenomenal lesson. When the big day finally came around, I was ready — dressed to impress with a starched shirt, matching tie, and a fresh haircut.

I made the typical rookie mistake of "prepping" my students for the event. I got them to promise to be on their best behavior with a lethal combination of bribery and guilt trips. I even remember telling them I could get fired if it didn't go well (*Never do this — it is just plants a seed in their minds!*). The day finally came, and it was go time. Naturally, I was greeting students at the door with a smile when a student informed me his locker was jammed. I quickly left to help him and returned to a crowd of rowdy students surrounding my door. Only one thing could draw that kind of crowd. Sure enough, I busted through the barricade of students only to discover what I had suspected from the first moment I arrived on the scene, *a fight*. As I rushed in to intervene, I thought to myself, "It can't get any worse than this to start an observation." *I was wrong.* No sooner than I conceived that thought, I glanced across the circle and saw that my administrator had arrived a few minutes *early*...just in time to help me break up the fight taking place in my doorway! To add insult to injury, we had recently been reminded as a staff of the importance of watching the hallways from our classroom doors.

Fortunately, my administrator escorted the boys to the office, so I had a few minutes to regain my composure and my students' attention. I tried everything I could to squelch the surging wave of testosterone that had washed over my classroom. The students were in a frenzy talking about the fight, and I knew that more than a few minor tweaks would be necessary to save this lesson. Maybe it was a vision of myself searching through the want ads looking for a new job or the adrenaline coursing through my veins after breaking up a fight, but I began to yell at my class for what just occurred (which was kind of silly since *they* weren't the ones involved in the fight). Finally, after *I* calmed down, I made one final pitch for them to save my tail by acting like angels.

And did they ever. They were perfect little angels the entire period, but I never knew angels were so quiet! I couldn't get anyone to say a word...*at all!* Everyone knows the feeling of doing an observation and tossing out questions to an audience that acts like it isn't even breathing. You could hear a pin drop the entire class period, even when I attempted to engage them in the learning process. They all would have received an "F" for participation. I was convinced that I would receive an "F" as well (except mine would stand for *Find another occupation*).

After all the dust settled, it was time for judgment day — my post conference. I was surprised in more ways than one. First off, he was impressed with the way I handled the fight, and with my classroom management (of course it is not too difficult to manage manikins), but the biggest surprise of all came in the areas I received criticism.

He *could have* pointed out that: my lesson had no opening or closing (unless you count the fight), there was no clear learning target, my students behaved like pre-programmed zombies, or any number of things. But he didn't. Instead, he communicated that he was really disappointed that I did not have a clearly displayed "Word Wall" in my classroom.

As I am sure you can guess, at the beginning of the school year we were all told that the latest research had shown that focusing on vocabulary through the use of a word wall was likely to result in drastic improvements in test scores. In typical male fashion, I wrote "Word Wall" on the corner of my dry erase board and placed that unit's vocabulary words beneath it. Seemed good enough to me. Evidently, some other teachers in the building had shown a little more creativity.

So that was the fatal flaw in my lesson—oh yeah, and I said "Christmas break" instead of "Winter break." Other than these colossal shortcomings, my lesson appeared to be just fine—even though it opened with a fight, focused on no discernible target, and caused my students to enter some odd state of hibernation for an entire class period. Apparently, I was only a word wall away from hitting it out of the park! I couldn't decide if I should be happy or upset with the way things turned out.

Though I didn't know it at the time, this was a good introduction to the strange animal of observations. *After all, teachers aren't the only ones who experience stress concerning observations.* Think of it from your administrator's perspective. Think it is easy to walk into someone's classroom, judge the lesson, and give feedback that you know may not be well received? Who knows, maybe my first administrator was just being nice and didn't want to obliterate a brand new teacher on his first observation that had the unfortunate occurrence of opening with a fight? *Any way you look at it, evaluations are tough (and getting tougher) for both teachers and administrators.*

To help you survive this ever evolving rite of passage for educators, we offer a few tips that we believe will stand the test of time and work well regardless of the latest educational trends and evaluation models.

Teach like you always teach. You won't fool a soul. Everyone, meaning the students *and* the evaluator, will know if you move away from your regular routine. The students won't know what to do because they have never done it before, and administrators have seen enough classrooms to easily recognize a "dog and pony show." I (Rob) once had a student teacher try something totally new only to have a frustrated student say out loud during his observation: "We've *never* done this before."

If you try to create good habits and good lessons day in and day out, then an observation is a lot less foreboding. Like my (Scotty) Drill Sergeant used to say, "We sweat in training, so we don't bleed in combat." *Do what you should be doing so that when it counts, nothing has to be changed.* Sweat so that you don't bleed. I hope you see that I am speaking metaphorically here—no one will actually be bleeding at the end of a bad observation…unless you open your lesson with a fight!

Prepping your students often backfires. I (Scotty) mentioned earlier that I made a rookie mistake of prepping my students for my first observation. What I mean by this is that all manners of bribery, guilt trips, and extortion may seem like good ideas to ease your anxiety about an upcoming observation, but they often find a way to come back and bite you in the end (like my classroom full of zombies).

First of all, a classroom full of students pretending just feels phony. We underestimate our administrators if we think they can't tell when our students are faking it. How does this behavior reflect on you if your classroom only looks good when everyone is pretending? When I (Rob) was in college, a fellow student teacher was asked by one of her students (as the observing professor was exiting the room): "Since we were good today does that mean we get to have a party tomorrow like you said?" Needless to say, her post-conference didn't go too smoothly!

It can be wise to inform your students about an upcoming evaluation and remind them that you expect excellence (as you always do), but try to spend more time prepping your lesson than your students!

Over-prepare so you don't under-perform. Always have more than you need for an observation. Then, when technology crashes (because we all know it loves to betray us at our most vulnerable moments!), or a fire drill cuts things short, you can adapt on the fly. Idle students — bad for classroom management. Idle students when you have an administrator in your classroom — bad for your career.

Don't try too hard. It can be tempting to try and throw all the latest and greatest buzzwords and activities into your lesson, but don't overdo it. It certainly doesn't hurt to add a few slants towards whatever educational strategy is popular at the moment, but remember that too much of a good thing ends up being a bad thing. As stated earlier, create good habits that will work any day, not just evaluation day.

No one is perfect. Recognize that it is your administrator's *job* to find ways to help you become a better teacher. In other words, *they* <u>have</u> <u>to</u> *suggest ways for you to improve.* Don't walk into a post conference expecting to hear: "Great job, I wouldn't change a thing." Accept criticism professionally.

Contrary to popular belief, the goal of observations is <u>not</u> to fool your evaluator. The goal is to teach a good lesson that represents a daily sample of your class, and then identify weak areas. If you make habits out of teaching well, personal reflection, and correcting weaknesses, then evaluations are nothing to fear. Obviously, the better you teach *without* an administrator in your room, the easier it is to teach *with* one in your room.

Taking a stand?

"Hell hath no fury like a <u>teacher</u> *scorned."*
- Not Shakespeare

This chapter has mentioned everything from policy changes, to political pressure, to the constant flux of professional development. In this context, we want to make a simple but crucial point:

In education, very few mountains are worth dying on.

Sooner or later, you will run into a shift in procedures, policies, or expectations that rubs you the wrong way. Further still, you will eventually face a situation with a student, parent, or administrator that has the same effect.

What do you do when you find yourself in such a place? *Many times a teacher has to lose to win.* By this we mean that you have to lose battles (even if you are fully convinced you are in the right) in order to win the war (make a difference in kid's lives in your classroom). When you decide to take on school policy, fight for the "F" a student deserves, or draw a line in the sand with a parent, *you will all too often* <u>lose</u>. You *may* get your way, but more often than not you end up losing the argument, losing credibility, losing respect, or losing motivation (and these types of losses usually surpass any potential gains). More importantly,

142

your time, talent, and energy are diverted from your classroom and focused on your crusade against whatever it is you are trying to change. *In the grand scheme of things, it's rarely worth it.*

We aren't saying there are no mountains worth dying on in education—just very few. At times, it is a matter of integrity and character to take a stand. In those places, fight with conviction, confidence, and purpose. But before you dig your heels in to the ground, be *absolutely certain* that it is a battle worth fighting. It's kind of like swatting at a bee. You'd better be sure you're going to get it—*or else you're going to get stung!*

SUMMARY

When I (Scotty) was finishing my first year as an educator, one of my colleagues was retiring after more than thirty years in the profession. What is even more impressive than her years of service was how many people commented on how she gave teaching her all up to her very last day. When I asked her about this, she told me: "Scotty, ultimately it doesn't matter what anyone says about how you teach. The only people who *truly* know if you are a good teacher or not is yourself and your students. Keep your principals and parents happy, but *never forget that you are here for the kids.*" Though at times I find myself fantasizing about the day I will no longer care and coast to retirement (let he who is without sin cast the first stone!), I truly hope the same will be said of me.

Regardless of whether or not you agree with the newest ideas and implementations, your job is to make students as successful as they can be.

Good teaching never goes out of style.

When what you are doing in your classroom is working, you don't have to care as much about chasing the latest trends. To put it in the words of my former colleague: If you care more about kids than fitting in with the big wigs of education, everything else — *including observations* — will fall into place.

My Classroom, My Kingdom

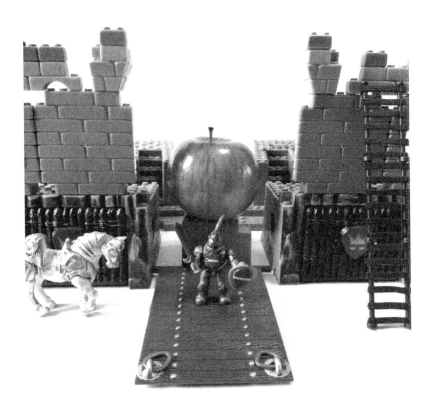

Chapter 10

Ruling well in your classroom, your school, and your community

"The buck stops here."

- Harry Truman

From 1945 to 1953 President Harry Truman kept a sign on his desk in the Oval Office that read: "The buck stops here." The saying originated as Truman's response to the infamous phrase, "Pass the buck" (meaning to pass responsibilities or blame on to someone else). It seems that the President believed whatever problems arose, *he* would have to be the one to fix them—no passing the buck on his watch.

What if we put that sign on our desks? Sure, there are a lot of reasons to complain about the state of education, but does any good *really* come from whining about it? To be completely honest, both of us have certainly done our fair share of griping over the years. But the longer we've been around, the more we've realized that sitting around talking about how it "used to be" or better yet, how it "should be" amounts to little more than a bad mood.

In this career, it is *way too easy* to pass the buck. Teachers searching for excuses can all too easily find somewhere to shift the blame: from impractical politicians, to bureaucratic school systems, to insufficient funding, to inept leadership, to irresponsible teachers passing on unprepared students, to flashy teachers making others look bad, to parents who let their children get away with anything, to students who couldn't care less. Teachers *looking for a reason* why their classroom can't be successful will never run short on places to pass the blame.

In a manner of speaking, one could argue that: "Because someone else isn't doing their job, I can't do mine." This is buck-passing at its best. The great irony is that buck passers are most frustrated by everyone else not doing what they are supposed to do. Stop and think about that. *Their chief complaint is other people shirking responsibilities, thereby passing the buck themselves.* Gather enough of these people together and nothing gets accomplished other than finger pointing and name calling. Sounds a little bit like modern day politics, doesn't it?!?

What we hope to set out here is a new way of viewing your career—how to be a buck stopper. The education system in America has its share of teachers who fill the faculty lounge with an endless list of excuses and perpetuate the cycle of passing blame. What this country *needs* is more teachers who have decided to let the buck stop at their classroom door. To do this, you must accept everything expected of you as an educator as *your* responsibility.

- *Your classroom is your kingdom...no matter what or where you teach.*
- *Your students are your citizens...no matter who they are or where they came from.*
- *Your school building is your nation...no matter who works there or how things work there.*
- *Your school community is part of your world...no matter what neighborhood your school calls home.*

Make it your job to <u>honor</u> each of these jurisdictions. Don't be one of the many who seem to think their responsibility is to *point out problems* (and sit around waiting for someone else to fix them). Choose to be one of the few who get about the business of *solving problems*. Remember, the buck stops at *your* door.

Your kingdom

"This is my house. I have to defend it."
- Kevin (Home Alone)

My (Rob) literal first day on the job taught me one of the most important lessons I have ever learned as a teacher. It was an in-service day, and after bagels and an icebreaker, we immediately launched into a two hour training on how to break up fights and diffuse conflict (not exactly how I thought my teaching career would begin!). In the middle of explaining the procedure for calling an administrator and School Resource Officer to your room, my principal got off on a random tangent that would turn out to shape my career in a crucial way.

She pointed at the call button in the room (which buzzed the office) and said, "We are here for you no matter what. Please hear me: We will *always* back you up. *But,* I want you to know that *every single time you push that button your students think less of you.* Each time you have to call in for back up, their perception of your authority, control, and influence goes down a notch."

As I mulled over her words, I began to realize that she had made quite a profound statement. She was challenging us teachers to honestly ask ourselves: *"Whose* classroom is it...*really?"* Does it belong to you, to students, to parents, to politicians? Take a moment to ask yourself:

Who is the person ultimately responsible for the success or failure of your classroom?

My principal's statement forced me to decide right then and there: Am *I* going to take the responsibility for the outcome of my classroom, or am I going to pass the buck?

I certainly had my share of buck-passing excuses. I was teaching in an inner-city setting that presented a host of challenges to a new teacher. I taught eighth graders who, if they passed, would go to a high school that, at that time, had a *twenty eight* percent graduation rate. From gang fights to drug busts to sixth graders hosting their own version of Sex Ed. in the bathroom, it was hard to do anything other than pass the blame. In fact, that year two other brand spanking new teachers started at the school along with me. One quit in September, and the other threw in the towel halfway through October.

While I might like to think that I was successful because I had superior skills or engaging lessons, the reality is that I stayed the course simply because I embraced my principal's challenge to believe that my classroom would rise or fall on *me* (and I was certainly too stubborn to accept defeat!). Throughout my *entire* career as a teacher, some of my favorite students came from that first year—resilient, inspirational, and downright determined to beat the odds. If I had chosen to focus on all the reasons why I couldn't be successful, I would not have experienced the joy of seeing those students succeed.

We challenge you to do the same. We dare teachers to think of their classroom as their own little kingdom—their own domain in which the whole world depends on them. *You are king or queen of your castle. No policy or politician can take that away from you.* When all is said and done, *you* are the reason that your class will be a success or failure. It's on your shoulders.

When you decide to do this—to own your classroom and all that goes on inside its four walls—you have a different perspective. To quote another wise president, Theodore Roosevelt, we challenge teachers to:

"Do what you can, with what you have, where you are."

No excuses. No pointing fingers. You have got what you've got, and it is up to you to make the most of it. *Winners don't whine, they win.* Don't choose to focus on all the reasons why your classroom can't be successful. Instead, choose to believe that *you* are the reason your classroom *can* be a success. It's your kingdom. How will you rule?

Your nation

"Why can't we be friends? Why can't we be friends?"
— *War*

"Scotty, we need to tell you something. Please sit down."

Two of my colleagues approached me during plan with a "this is serious" look on their faces. Quickly, my mind began skimming over our conversations at lunch, and I tried to remember if I had said anything stupid. Drawing a blank, I sat down and waited to hear the news.

"Scotty, we need to tell you something about Ms. Lewis."

"Sure, what is it?"

"Well, it turns out that 'Samantha' is actually Sam."

"Say that again."

"The new math teacher, Ms. Lewis, is actually, well, *Mr.* Lewis."

"Excuse me?"

"Ms. Lewis is a man that dresses as a woman."

As I sat and absorbed the information just passed to me, it sunk in sort of like a climactic scene in a movie — one where you find out that a main character is *actually* a double agent and all of the sudden dozens of previous scenes finally make sense. Ms. Lewis *was* pretty tall. She *did* have a deep voice. She wore *a lot* of make-up. Honestly, I sat across the lunch table from her for months and never questioned her true identity. Some of my co-workers were evidently much more observant and well, inquiring minds want to know. One brave soul finally just asked Ms. Lewis if her suspicions were correct and he came out with the truth. Ms. Lewis was actually a mister.

Let's just say the next few months were *a little* awkward. I was already the only male eighth grade teacher *(or so I thought)*. I had no hate in my heart, but I also had *no idea* how to react. I had only been teaching for a couple years and must have played hooky in college the day they explained how to acclimate to a cross-dressing co-worker. To make matters worse, rumors started to spread that he had tight connections with a civil organization and was looking for a lawsuit.

The staff was duly instructed to give extra care not to discriminate, and the year continued on as normally as possible. As you could imagine, it was only a matter of time before the news made it to the student body. While the faculty handled the situation with professionalism, the students were a little less subdued. Regardless of your stance on transgender issues, you have to realize that middle schoolers don't care one bit about political correctness. All of us teachers found ourselves trying to diffuse statements like:

"Mr. Hicks, did you hear that Ms. Lewis is a dude?!?"

"Well I heard that Jeff's dad told him to call Ms. Lewis, *Mr.* Lewis from now on."

"My mom already put in for a transfer. There is no way *he* is going to teach me all year."

Not to mention that many of my students suddenly became Aerosmith's biggest fans. It seems I couldn't make it through a class change without hearing "Dude looks like a lady!" being sung somewhere in the hallways.

It was a trying time for my school. I was teaching in a very conservative, upscale community in Tennessee, and the news of a transgender teacher working with their children was not well received. In my mind, it was only a matter of time before this story stirred a national debate. However, much to my surprise, it didn't. The staff treated our new member with respect, and at the end of the temporary position for which he was hired (covering another teacher's maternity leave), he left. The end.

It has been many years since Mr. Lewis graced the halls of my previous placement, but the lessons I learned from that situation have served me well over my teaching career. Regardless of their personal convictions and feelings about the issue, *the faculty put the school and the students first.* I saw how important and how powerful it was for a staff to put personal issues to the side, do what was best for the community, and focus on what we were all there to do in the first place — *teach!*

While many teachers have not had the experience of a cross-dressing co-worker, we have all found ourselves in situations where the unity and community of our staff is at risk (for one reason or another). We've spent a while trying to convince you to see your classroom as your own little kingdom, but as I'm sure you've noticed, you aren't the only monarch in the big castle. In fact, you are surrounded by many other kings and queens and divided only by cinder blocks. What should you make of this? *How should your classroom and your role as a teacher fit into the grand scheme of your school?* We think it would be best explained with a little history lesson...

Everyone remembers learning about ancient Greece. From Homer, to the Parthenon, to the beginnings of democracy, to Socrates and Plato, to the Olympic games, it seems that ancient Greece has something interesting to offer everyone who takes the time to listen. However, lesser known is the story of how Greece got to be so remarkable — how it got to be all the things for which it is so famous.

It all began with city-states that did anything but get along peacefully. They were bitter rivals and competed constantly. None more famously than the two leading powers: Sparta and Athens. These two city-states were fierce rivals, and in many regards, were complete and total

153

opposites.

The Spartans were men's men, not quite as fierce as they were in the movie *300*...but close. They were military fanatics that trained for war straight out of the womb, drank blood, and chewed on nails (only kidding...sort of). Their culture was built on courage, sweat, and strength. The Spartans got things done.

The Athenians preferred brains over brawn. They wrote poems, dabbled with democracy, and created cultural icons that top the list even today. Their lifeblood was found in philosophy, intellect, and art. The Athenians just might have been the sharpest tools in the shed.

These two city-states couldn't stand each other (and it's easy to see why), *and then something strange happened.* The city-states came under attack. Xerxes and his conquering empire of Persia came with force to squash the Greek city-states. All of a sudden, Sparta and Athens didn't have much choice. *In the interest of self-preservation, they united and somehow managed to find a way to defeat a far more powerful enemy.* In the years that followed, Greece experienced an explosion of culture, success, peace, and prosperity (and created many of the things for which they are so famous).

In many ways, our schools aren't much different. We have Spartans—teachers who don't tolerate excuses, get things done, hold the line, straighten out the tough kids, maintain structure, and eat the cafeteria food. We also have Athenians—teachers who dream, innovate, reflect, love to read professional development books, and regularly experience those strange things called feelings.

Guess what? *We are at war.* Whether you realize it or not, we are fighting a war for the hearts and minds of our students...*and we need each other.* It is not enough just to recognize that there are different personalities in the building (as we mentioned in a previous chapter). Those different personalities have to *choose to set aside their differences,* learn to support each other, and work together for the good of everyone in the castle, eh, school. We won't win this war if we are fighting (or gossiping!) amongst ourselves along the way. Whether we are from Sparta, Athens, or anywhere in between, *we are stronger together than apart.*

This section has been laced pretty heavily with metaphors so let us give it to you plain and simple: *Get along.* Chances are you work with some people you don't like: People who are very different from you, people who have done and said things they shouldn't, people who have a totally different teaching style than your own, and some people who, frankly, should have changed careers long ago (though unfortunately they haven't and most likely never will). That being said, you still need to maintain professional, supportive, and positive relationships if you want to win the war at your school. Make *friends.* This doesn't mean that you have to invite your colleagues over to your house for a family picnic. *It simply means that you look for something to appreciate in every one of your colleagues because you value working in a positive environment.* It's a lot more fun to work with friends than enemies.

Of course, "playing well with others" is easier said than done. A great deal of drama swarms around schools...and we are *not* just talking about the kids! Here are a few suggestions that may improve the working environment of your school:

<u>Do</u>

Be positive. You can't change a co-worker's attitude, but you can change yours. Be positive and it will help other teachers do the same.

Surround yourself with positive teachers. We know the best advice for getting along with some co-workers is to keep your distance, but this certainly isn't true for most of the teachers in your school. Surround yourself with those who are encouraging to their students and their colleagues.

Help each other. Every school day is unpredictable. One minute you are sailing smoothly, the next minute you are inside a hurricane of chaos. This is why we desperately need each other's support. Helping another teacher (even in the simplest of ways) is one of the best ways to create positive working relationships and a supportive culture.

Don't

Don't gossip. Kids aren't the only ones whispering in the halls during class change. Do your part to keep juicy rumors at bay.

"If you don't have anything nice to say, don't say anything at all." This golden nugget dished out by mommas for decades works well everywhere—especially in a school setting. Criticism and negativity can destroy the culture in your school one comment at a time. This is especially true when talking to students about other teachers.

Don't complain. Whining only has one effect—*more whining* (sort of like watching someone yawn). Watch your words because a complaint can tear through a school building faster than a stomach virus. We all need to vent every now and again, but try to purge the tanks to an outsider (like a spouse or close friend).

If we truly want our students to cut down on all the drama, we must first practice what we preach. You will certainly have a few people that will test your optimism with remarkable persistence, but fighting for a positive culture and friendly relations with your co-workers is well worth it. *Treat others the way you want to be treated (despite how they treat you).* No excuses, the buck stops at your door.

Your allies

As we all know, a school is made up of much more than teachers and students. Many important positions are required to effectively and efficiently run a school, and each has the power to dramatically disrupt or ensure the success of any given school day. Principals, secretaries, custodians, cafeteria ladies (why are there never any cafeteria men?); *everyone* in the building plays a crucial role.

Administrators: Your principals have a tough job. They have to evaluate, support, and hold accountable all of the teachers in the building, stay up to date with local, state, and federal legislation (which are constantly changing), deal with the most difficult parents and students, represent the community, show up at numerous concerts, plays, and athletic events, lead professional development sessions, attend awards ceremonies and photo ops, drive all over the state going to various trainings, strictly adhere to school board policy, manage the physical and fiscal logistics of the school, keep an eye on morale, and oh yeah, they are usually evaluated solely on how well *we* do our job! Put yourself in their shoes for a moment: double your responsibilities, triple your stress levels, and subtract summer break.

Very similar to armchair coaches (fans supposing they could do a better job coaching their favorite team), some teachers believe they could run the school better than their administration (and just like the fans, often have zero leadership experience). *We challenge you to support the leadership in your school building.* Principals need your support as much as you need theirs. This doesn't mean being a "yes man" (or woman) and folding up every ounce of personal conviction. This doesn't mean brown-nosing and kissing up. It simply means working together. Have the humility and maturity to realize that your job will be *a whole lot easier* if you have a positive, respectful, and professional relationship with your boss. *Make allies with*

157

your administration.

Support staff: Greeting visitors, answering phones, and constantly communicating with everyone in the building, support staff are the gatekeepers (*and bookkeepers!*) to every kingdom in the building. They are dealing with numerous stresses of their own and deserve your kindness and patience. Treat them well and your kindness will not go unnoticed. *Make allies with your support staff.*

Maintenance: You don't realize how crucially important the custodian is until someone pukes in your room, you're A/C unit breaks, or you notice a few seconds too late that the toilet paper roll is out! I (Scotty) once had a Vietnamese custodian who spoke very little English, but as the weeks went by, we slowly began to communicate. One day I asked him what he did back in Vietnam, and he replied: "Doctor." *What? Did he say doctor?* My principal confirmed that the man sweeping my floors was a medical doctor (he could not practice in the United States due to regulations and certification requirements). I tell this story for one simple reason—*treat everyone with dignity and respect.* Who knows, *your* janitor might turn out to be lawyer!?! *Make allies with maintenance.*

Every person that works in a school building has an important role to play. From teaching assistants to custodians to cafeteria workers, everyone matters. Treat everyone who works in your building as a crucial member of the team. In other words, *make allies with everyone.* Doing so creates an environment in which everyone wants to work...and don't tell anyone we told you this...but it also helps you get extra food in the cafeteria line!

Your world

A pencil is snapped in half and then violently flung to the floor. A flushed face, with veins bulging, explodes into a tirade of "correctional suggestions" complete with an occasional insertion of profanity. A class sits in silence as they watch their teacher lose all sense of self-control. They don't move a muscle in hopes of avoiding any individual focus of their instructor's fury—all except for one student who manages to slip his phone out of his pocket and record the unfortunate incident. Before the bell rings, the entire episode is posted for the world to see on YouTube.

You work in a "public" school, and the wonders of technology have only increased just how *public* the events of our classroom can become. Spend a few minutes searching the Internet and you will find dozens of videos captured by students of their teachers losing their temper, putting them to sleep, or commenting unprofessionally on politics, social issues, and religion.

If you want to run your kingdom well, you have to give due attention to public relations. The most obvious application of this—and one where some teachers fail miserably—is to choose your words carefully when talking about your students or your school out in the community. With astonishing frequency, teachers vocalize how they "really feel" at the baseball field, grocery store, or hair salon, only to have their words come back to haunt them. *Speaking negatively of your school or students benefits no one, but choosing to speak positively of them benefits everyone.*

There is a lot you can do get some good press for your school. I (Rob) like to use a strategy one of my friends in college called "staying ahead of the curve." A bunch of guys had decided to go camping when one of my friends, recently engaged, announced that he had figured out how to keep his darling fiancée happy. Curious at this most recent stride forward into the mystery of the inner workings of the female mind, we all listened intently to his theory. He went on to explain how to stay ahead of the curve:

Scenario A: A man driving home from work spontaneously picks up a dozen roses for his wife. He surprises her with the bouquet, and all is good on the home front. A few days later, he totally forgets to do anything to celebrate their anniversary.

Scenario B: A man is told by his wife one night that he had totally forgotten to celebrate their anniversary that day. Driving home from work the next day, he stops to get a dozen roses to apologize.

Who is in *more* trouble (and no ladies, you can't say both of them!)? They both bought flowers and both forgot their anniversary, but most would agree that the man in scenario A will spend less time sleeping on the couch than the man in scenario B. Why? He was staying ahead of the curve.

What in the world does this have to do with teaching? Teachers should also stay ahead of the curve by being proactive when it comes to their interaction with their community. You as a teacher and your students in your classroom have a "relationship" with, not only the rest of the school, but the community as a whole. In a manner of speaking, *you are an ambassador for your school in your community.* Since we have been discussing modern and historical politics, let's take some liberty with another famous presidential quote: *"Ask not what your school can do for you, but ask what you can do for your school."*

How can you as a teacher pick up a dozen roses on your way home from work (metaphorically speaking of course!)? What can you do to show that you care, and want to see your students, your school, and yourself look good in the community? Though the percentage of husbands spontaneously buying roses on the way home from work may indicate that this is an *extremely* difficult thing to do, it's really not that hard! There are countless opportunities for you and your students that are as easy to find as the local grocery store. A teacher who wants to be a good ambassador of their school will always:

160

Be on the look out for things that will give your school and students positive recognition.

There are many contests, competitions, honors societies, newspaper journalists searching for articles to write, service projects waiting to be done, or news programs looking to fill gaps with local stories. Sadly, it seems that when schools get mentioned in the news it is almost always negative. From a system cutting jobs to a student and teacher having an "inappropriate" relationship, there is no shortage of bad press for today's schools. Strive to reverse that trend — to be newsworthy in a positive way. It's a simple way to show your students, your administration, and your community that you *care* and are making a difference.

We'd like to pretend that being somewhat of a public figure is perfect, neat, and clean, but we must also discuss the less glorious side of being an ambassador. We might not have the paparazzi on our tail, but teachers are constantly under scrutiny from their community. People watch what you say, what you wear, what you order, what you purchase, what movie you attend, and on, and on (not to mention what teachers *voluntarily* publicize on the Internet!).

If teachers were perfect people, this would be no concern. But since we are bound to mess up, say something dumb, or be somewhere a parent doesn't think we should be (though they only see us if *they are there* too!), we need to be prepared. I once heard a minister say, *"We are all one decision away from stupid,"* and the following example is certainly proof of just that!

I (Scotty) once compared a slacking student to a "turd," and a rumor is floating out there that I may have on a separate occasion called another misbehaving student a "dingle-berry." Oddly, when a mother called asking if teachers were allowed to call their students turds or dingle-berries, my administrator did not have my back. *Oops.* It was a slip up, a momentary lapse of judgment messing with a couple of delinquent students.

Fortunately, my ill-chosen attempt to motivate was cushioned by a long trend of staying ahead of the curve—a track record of caring about students and being a positive representative of our school. My principal didn't come down too hard on me because my previous actions proved that my slip up was just that, a slip up. But what if my track record showed something different? What if my work in the classroom said I didn't care about my students or my school? What if it said I did think they were all a bunch of turds? A history like that could have cost me my job.

We can't do anything to change the fact that our community is watching us and holding us to a much higher standard than they hold themselves. It's just a part of teaching. We can *try* to be perfect, never make a mistake, and never say or do anything that would offend anyone, but as you know all too well, the stress of teaching causes even the best of us to mess up. Stay ahead of the curve. Show that you care, and create some cushion for your inevitable slip ups as you take on the impossible task of never making a mistake.

SUMMARY

"Win the crowd, and you will win your freedom."
                    - Proximo (Gladiator)

Every teacher has a choice: You are either a helpless serf hampered by all that is against a modern day educator, or you are a king or queen whose classroom is a kingdom for which you are ultimately responsible.

Let the success or failure of your teaching career be your fault.

Leave the excuse-making to your students. Your classroom is your kingdom. What are you going to do with it? The buck stops with *you*.

All that being said, a wise ruler will refuse to attempt this alone. There is a famous scene in the movie *Gladiator* where Proximo explains to Maximus that he was a great gladiator not just because of how he fought—but because he learned how to win the crowd. He promises Maximus: "Win the crowd, and you will win your freedom." This is perfect advice for teachers (and not just because we have all taught classes that made us feel like a gladiator fighting for our life in the Roman Coliseum!). Proximo's words remind us that there is another layer to being a great teacher—winning the crowd. We are gravely mistaken if we believe that standing up in front of class and teaching is the *only* thing that matters. We have to <u>win</u> the respect, appreciation, and trust of our students, administration, co-workers, support staff, parents, and community. Speak well of others, and they will speak well of you. Support others, and they will support you. *Win the crowd.*

164

Leaving a legacy that goes beyond learning

How does a teacher go from good to great? *The difference between a good teacher and a great teacher has almost nothing to do with instruction (Yes, we really just said that!).* Take a moment to reflect on the best teacher you ever had. Ask others about theirs. Chances are you will hear very little (if anything) about riveting pedagogy or effective assessments. You won't hear: "Mrs. Thomas was my favorite teacher—her lesson on polynomials was so inspirational!" No, you won't hear *anything* like that. People will recall a teacher who encouraged them, built their confidence, pointed their life in a different direction, stood up for them, connected with them during a time of difficulty, or challenged them to become something more than they were before. The remaining chapters will have very little to do with instruction because *great teachers not only instruct, they inspire.*

Encourage or End-Courage?

Chapter 11

Embracing the power of encouragement

"How do you know if a child needs encouragement? If he or she is breathing."

- Truett Cathy

Most people in the small southern town of Sweetwater, Tennessee thought I (Scotty) was destined for anything that did not require a high school diploma, and I have to admit that I wouldn't have disagreed with their prediction. I was fortunate to grow up in a stable and loving home. My parents worked hard but were uneducated. Neither of them graduated from high school. As a matter of fact, my father, Ben Hicks quit school in the *seventh grade* at the age of *sixteen*. Yes, you read it correctly, I said *sixteen*. Do the math. He was held back...*a lot.*

Born into poverty—along with *thirteen* brothers and sisters—my father didn't exactly thrive in the academic climate of the 1940s and 50s. If he attended school today, he would probably be coded with more acronyms than a top secret government agency. You know what I mean—ADD, ADHD, in need of an IEP, but more on that later. After quitting school, he worked random labor jobs around town and within a couple of years, he was married. Just like that, two teenagers from East Tennessee had tied the knot. As one might expect, the marriage lasted less than a year.

Upset with his failed marriage, my father decided to leave Sweetwater and never look back. In what almost appears to be a secret attempt to eventually sell his life story to Hollywood, my father decided to join the circus *(seriously)*. The show had just left town, and all he had to his name was a tattered circus flyer showing its schedule of stops. On a mission to catch up, he hitchhiked east hoping to intersect the circus at a show in Washington D.C. A few weeks later he arrived in D.C. only to find out the circus was actually performing in Washington...*state*. With a stubborn persistence that seemed to define my father's life, he held out his thumb and headed west.

Two years and many stories later, including: arrests for vagrancy, a ride from burglars of a liquor store, and sleeping in ditches, my father finally made it to the other side of the continent and hooked up with a circus in California. He traveled the country with the circus selling popcorn and Coke—except for the time he had to stand in for the *Incredible Snake Tamer*. (Maybe substitute teachers could relate?) Life became routine. You know, run of the mill kind of stuff: traveling with circus acts, sleeping above the rattlesnake containers, and dodging monkey poop, but something, or should I say *someone*, was about to change everything.

At a show stop in the small town of Ironton, Ohio, my father met a pretty young lady in the audience who began to consume his thoughts. Though he continued to travel with the circus, it seemed his heart remained in Ironton. Writing letters every week only fueled the fire. Before he knew it, young Ben was hitch-hiking toward another dream, back to Ironton, and back to my mother.

Amazingly, my mom was also born into poverty along with twelve siblings, and similarly, quit school before graduating. Wooed by an exciting young man from the circus with tales of worldly travels, my parents married within months. Two years and one kid later (my older brother), my parents were hard pressed to make ends meet. When a letter from his cousin informed my father that the steel foundry in Sweetwater was hiring, they packed up and headed south. He was hired, and soon thereafter, I was born.

My humble beginnings began with an older brother, who mostly viewed me as the annoying little sibling (though we are close now); a mother who loved her kids tenderly, but let them roam as far as their bicycles would take them; and a loving, but circus carny father who collected aluminum cans and ate squirrel every chance he could get. While this might come as a complete surprise, *academia was not a high priority in my home.* The only thing I can remember from my childhood to steer me towards success in school was being given a summer membership to the city pool if I passed each grade. My future consisted of a hope and expectation that, if I was lucky, I would end up with an entry position in one of the local factories. Good honest work for good honest pay. But something would happen that would change my destiny.

At some point in junior high school I transitioned from being an "okay" student to being a lazy, unmotivated, and uninspired student. During my freshman year in high school, I actually began to fail classes. As a teacher, I have seen plenty of parents who have high expectations for their child's academic achievement and future economic success, but run short on love. I, it seemed, experienced the opposite. My parents sincerely loved and cared for me (and for that I am truly thankful), but they didn't exactly help structure my life towards success. As a teenager trying to find his place, outside of the honor roll that is, I sought attention any way I could get it.

I began skateboarding, break-dancing, driving a low-rider truck, and listening to rap music. Today, these things are viewed as typical teenage behavior, but in the 1980s in a small rural town in East Tennessee, I broke the mold to say the least. I also did plenty of things in the classroom to get noticed: disrespecting teachers, goofing off, sleeping, and refusing to do homework. My eleventh grade U.S. history teacher (the subject I now teach!) gave me a "circled 70" for my final grade. It was a polite way to say I failed the class, but she couldn't bear the thought of seeing me on her roster next school year. As if my knee high Chuck Taylors, Hammer pants, and long bleach-blonde mullet hybrid hair-do didn't drop a big enough hint, I was *desperate* for someone to notice me.

Lost, I decided to join the track team on a whim. I had a coach who told us at our first practice that he didn't know anything about track. (Maybe he was the only teacher who wasn't tenured when the position came open? No, something like that would *never* happen in a public school!) As luck would have it, my friend's dad, Hugh "Doc" McCampbell, helped out with the team. As a forty-something year old who could out-run half of the track team, he immediately gained my respect. Little did I know the man would change my life forever.

Shockingly, our twelve member track team never won a meet, and although I did place a couple times, I never won a race. As the season went on, I enjoyed track but found it to be another place where I wasn't finishing first. Then, it happened.

Doc McCampbell unexpectedly came to my
house to brag about me to my parents.

We were all kind of dumbstruck when he showed up at our house, knocked a couple of times, and then let himself in the front door. (If I remember right, my mom was wearing her night gown!) My parents had never even been to one of my races, but Doc didn't miss a beat when he told them all about my newfound abilities: "I am telling you Mr. and Mrs. Hicks, your son is good, *real* good. If he keeps this up, he will have a scholarship by the time he graduates. You should be *very* proud."

And they were, but not as much as I. No one had ever bragged on me like that before, especially in front of my

170

parents. It changed something inside of me. *He made me believe that I was a runner.* He also planted a seed in me that I might actually be able to attend college one day. And all of this happened in less than ten minutes worth of encouragement. Thanks to Doc, a new courage began to rise up within me.

Fast forward several years and that boy — born into poverty to parents who didn't graduate high school in a county often noted more for its high percentage of teen pregnancies and meth labs than its humble and friendly residents, eventually breaks his slacking habits and serves an eleven year honorable military career, obtains four college degrees with a 3.8 average G.P.A., gains a professional career in one of the top performing schools in the state, and wins numerous teaching awards. I am an author whose father never read an entire book! How is this possible? I can honestly say, it is _not_ because of me. It only became possible because of Doc McCampbell and other people like him. It only became possible because of the power of encouragement.

My story certainly is unique, but doesn't everyone have barriers to overcome? Doesn't every kid eventually face difficult circumstances (internally and externally)? *My life started taking a different path simply because someone cared enough to encourage me.* Sometimes I wonder where I would be today if Doc McCampbell never stopped by my house or took an interest in me.

Sometimes I wonder how my father's life could have turned out if he had teachers, coaches, or other adults that encouraged him — people who actually believed he could end up doing something other than getting hitched as a teenager and running away to join the circus. Many parts of my father's story certainly are humorous. After all, how could you *not* smile at a jolly old squirrel-eating soul from the backwoods (think *Duck Dynasty*)? On the other hand, his lack of education, troubled youth, and unstructured upbringing led him to becoming divorced, homeless, and stuck in many undesirable situations. Thankfully, with a little luck, a bit of stubbornness, and *a ton* of heart and courage, my father was able to improve his lot in life (but not without difficult times for him and his family). When I think of all he managed to accomplish without someone believing in him, I can only imagine how much more he could have done if someone had.

While the stories of individuals who have risen above humble and challenging beginnings are numerous, there are many more young men and women who live up to the sad expectations laid out for their life: quitting school, living off of government assistance, or featured in the local papers because of their run-in with the law. The ones who make it, who rise above and beat the odds, have a common theme:

Somewhere, some how, someone began building them up.

While teaching students like my former self or my father is full of numerous challenges, I can't help but be inspired to think that I could be some lost child's "Doc McCampbell," that I could be a kid's sole *(and soul)* encourager, that some punk kid without a prayer might be writing a book twenty years from now about the day Mr. Hicks "stopped by his house."

Encourage

After all of my life's experiences, I (Scotty) have developed a few principles to remind myself to unleash the power of encouragement in my classroom. The difference these ideas can make is astounding. First:

Encourage your students and encourage them often.

It sounds almost too simple, but I promise that if you do this regularly and sincerely, your students will:

- Smile
- Begin to like you
- Be more likely to behave
- *Want* to do well for you (even during standardized testing!)
- Feel guilty when they do let you down
- Occasionally even encourage *you* in return

It really is that simple. *All you have to do is to let them know when they do something well* (you'd be amazed how many students *don't* have someone encouraging them at home). So encourage your students and encourage them often. Even when you are correcting them, find a way to encourage. If at all possible, find a way to do it in front of others. It may take some serious searching, but sooner or later, you can catch *every* student doing something well.

Recently, I have begun the adventure of helping coach my own kids' sports teams. My "only wears pink, carries babies everywhere she goes, delicate, but energetic" little daughter, Bella, took an interest in playing soccer when she was four. However, we quickly found out that she was *much more* interested in picking the flowers on the field for her mommy than she was kicking the soccer ball. After surrendering to the reality that a soccer scholarship wasn't likely in Bella's future, I set progressive goals for her throughout the season. Goal one: make it through a game without crying. Goal two: actually try to touch the ball. Goal three: don't touch the ball with your hands. As a competitive father I wanted to pull my hair out, but as her daddy, I kept looking for ways to encourage her.

"Honey, I am so proud of you! You made it through the whole game without crying!"

"I know Daddy, but I got my pink cleats all dirty. Here, have a flower."

The competitor in me wanted to scream but the encourager won out, and I ended up coaching most games with a flower in my ear. That season did not turn her into a soccer star, but she did improve and had a great time "playing" the game.

We firmly believe teachers can transform their classroom with the power of encouragement, but before we head to the teacher supply store and stock up on stickers, certificates, and trophies, there is one catch: *You can't fake it.* The only way this will truly work in your classroom is to actually mean what you say.

Encouragement must be sincere.

Everyone has experienced "un-couragement." This happens when compliments are lavished upon you without an ounce of conviction.

We have all felt the pride and joy that comes from a thoughtless compliment. After all, we live in a society where kids get trophies, not for winning, but for participating (my daughter's soccer team *all* received trophies, even though they barely won a game). That is great for little kids, but as kids get older, praise must be genuine to be effective. *If everyone is a champion, no one actually feels like a champion.* To truly empower a student, we have to encourage something worthy of attention— something they earned.

Encouragement vs. Expectation

It's easy to write off the responsibility to be encouraging as *soft*—a "warm-fuzzy" feeling that doesn't help students in the long run. In fact, some teachers believe authentically encouraging students is the opposite of challenging them.

In other words, a teacher has to choose between helping a student feel better or holding them to high expectations. This couldn't be further from the truth. Offering your students real encouragement does *not* require sacrificing your desire to stretch them with high expectations.

My (Scotty) experiences at basic training in Fort Knox, Kentucky taught me this principle in a very painful way. My Drill Sergeants (*who were anything but soft, warm, and fuzzy!*) were experts at encouragement. Their preferred method of "encouraging" was making my arms feel like jello:

- Didn't put on your hat immediately when you stepped outside? *"Beat your face Private Hicks!"* (do push-ups)
- Didn't take off your hat immediately when you went inside? *"Kiss mother earth Hicks!"* (do more push-ups)
- Didn't eat all of your chow in five minutes? *"Front Leaning Rest Position, Move!"* (and more)
- Breathing a Drill Sergeant's oxygen? *"Drop and give me all you can and then give me twenty more!"*

I think you get the picture. Sometimes I wish I could use this method in the classroom! I actually tried it once and promptly was "encouraged" by my principal to discontinue the practice immediately.

While my Drill Sergeants did a lot of breaking us down, there was a method to their madness. They weren't just trying to make us feel depressed and miserable about ourselves, they were trying to push us beyond our limits — to exceed our own expectations. They wanted us to *earn* our encouragement. As a matter of fact, before I could even get up from a grueling round of push-ups, I had to ask for permission in a very specific manner: "Drill Sergeant! Thank you for conditioning my mind, body, and soul. Please feel free to do so at all times! Private Hicks requests permission to re-cov-er!" At this point, I would usually have to do some more *very sloppy* push-ups, and when my arms felt weaker than a wet noodle, they would finally let me stand up.

Mind, body, and soul. Think about that for a minute. A lot more than push-ups was going on when I was "kissing mother earth." They wanted us to work hard, get results, and earn our stripes. They wanted us to know that there was a deeper level to this process (though honestly, at the time, all I could think about was my sore muscles). However, as the weeks passed, I became less and less sore, and the Drill Sergeants did a little less pointing out our inabilities and a little more pointing out where and how we had improved. It was nice getting a compliment from them because when they gave you one, you knew it was *real*. You knew you accomplished something worth being recognized.

In basic training, I never received praise for my shooting abilities (because I shoot slightly better than Dick Cheney), but my superiors would often compliment my speed by saying something tender and uplifting like: "#$&^@!#! Private Hicks! You run faster than a gerbil being chased by a honey badger!" Believe it or not, compliments like that actually made me want to run faster. *My experiences in the Army taught me that it is possible to be encouraging and hold someone to a high standard at the same time.*

If all we ever do is encourage, it's flattery. If all we ever do is hammer kids with expectations, it's battery. *It's the combination of the two, just the right balance of encouragement and expectation, that transforms lives.* If we learn how to do this with our students like the Army does with its soldiers — okay, maybe not *exactly* like my Drill Sergeants — but if we offer our students *real* compliments that come as a result of accomplishing *realistic* expectations, we will begin to unleash the power of "in-couragement."

In-Courage

Everyone benefits from being encouraged. It sparks a change in attitude that begins to *create courage.* It literally empowers a person to stand "in-courage." Sincere encouragement from a meaningful adult helps kids *(and adults!)* be courageous enough to overcome difficult circumstances, courageous enough to try even though success may seem distant, and even courageous enough to accomplish things that at the outset seem impossible.

Famous American author Mark Twain once said: "I can live two months on a good compliment." *An unmistakable power flows out of meaningful praise.* If you are willing to catch students being successful and sincerely compliment them, you will unlock their desire to achieve. This brings us to our next principle.

Success breeds success.

No one wakes up successful. The only way someone can obtain long-term success is to build upon smaller successes earlier in life. In a very real way, *students' success in school will shape their attitude towards their own ability to be successful in life.* They have to experience some success in economics class to believe they can become an entrepreneur in the business world. They have to experience some success on the basketball court before they can confidently defend a case in a courtroom. They have to successfully spin their way out of a late homework assignment to launch a career in politics! There is great power in recognizing this concept. *Everything that happens in a classroom has the potential to affect each student's perception of their ability to achieve future success.*

I recall watching an interview during the 2012 Summer Olympics when a coach made a similar comment about his protégé: "Success breeds confidence." The athletes who compete at the Olympic level have won hundreds of competitions prior to the Olympics. They are confident in their abilities because they have a track record of success, but it is important for us to remember that they were not born Olympians (or confident for that matter). Every single one of them started out as an unskilled, untrained, unqualified, and inexperienced rookie...kind of like a first year teacher! But their parents and coaches recognized their unique talents and pushed them to learn and grow. They received the right combination of high expectations and sincere encouragement that culminated in winning, *and winning brought confidence.* With that confidence, they worked harder and won more, thus creating a cycle of success. Let's start trying to give our students some "wins" upon which to build. They may not end up in the Olympics, but they will start believing in themselves.

End-Courage

Unfortunately, the "cycle of success" isn't the only cycle we see spinning in our classrooms. The momentum can pull just as powerfully in the opposite direction.

Just as success breeds success, failure breeds failure.

Most of us have *some* students that tend to do more things wrong than right. Day after day, class after class, report card after report card, they fail (or squeak by with a "circled 70!"). As teachers, we know that most failing students are not giving it their best shot only to fall short. So let's be honest, many failures are just that, *failures* — apathetic, unmotivated, or unsupported and held unaccountable at home. As educators, we typically inherit these kids with more baggage than a commercial airline. But when they step in your room, you have a very serious choice to make.

What cycle will you perpetuate?

Will you add more weight to the momentum of their inevitable failure in life? Or will you build a few blocks on the successful side of things? Will you stretch yourself and risk catching them doing something right? Or are you *only* going to point out their failures? Think about it this way: *You are either encouraging your students to succeed or you are encouraging them to fail.* There isn't much room in between.

Choosing to heap a greater sense of failure on an unsuccessful student is something we like to call "end-couragement." Sadly, it seems that anyone who has spent a decent amount of time in school can point to a teacher who has perfected this art. You know what we are talking about. They are bitter, hate their job, and from the looks of things, hate kids. Cruel sarcasm, fear, and humiliation seem to bring them a secret joy as they try to grind out yet another day standing between themselves and retirement.

While most teachers aren't nearly so severe, we all need to work on our own sense of end-couragement. This doesn't mean we refuse to fail students. It doesn't mean we don't hold students accountable. It simply means we try our best to have all our students—even those who may fail our class—leave our room with a better sense of themselves than when they entered it. It's okay to fail students, just don't destroy them in the process.

Let us seek to be educators that build confidence in unsuccessful students and help them believe they might just be able to do something other than fail. We hope we will all become teachers who help students find just that—*hope*. Hope that they can rise above their circumstances and pursue a better future. Most students won't be transformed overnight, or even in one school year, but we believe that if, as a collective whole, teachers tried to build up instead of

179

tear down great strides could be made in even the most unlikely cases. I was a student bearing a heavy load, then Doc McCampbell and others like him started tipping the scales in a different direction.

Placing courage in the hearts of our students is powerful. It uplifts, inspires, and creates the desire for success. The more you do it, honestly and sincerely, the greater effect it will have. The success will breed confidence, which in the end will breed more success.

If you've been in the classroom a while, you may be tempted to pass all this off as just some new-age, hold hands and sing kumbaya, feel good fluff, but it has some very practical applications as well. Many of my (Scotty) students' test scores have improved simply because I have pulled them aside and let them know that they are more than a number on a test, or pointed out something other than academia where they excel. In a strange way, it almost makes them feel guilty for not giving it their all in the classroom. It doesn't always stick, but often it creates an avenue for them to prove to themselves and everyone involved in their lives that they have the ability to improve—that there is more to them than meets the eye. One of the most difficult tasks as a teacher (especially with older, struggling students) is simply getting them to *try*. But the numbers don't lie. If you can convince a student—some how, some way—to try their best they will *always* improve.

My experiences as a teacher and student have taught me that:

Meaningful encouragement is the most powerful tool a teacher has to make a lasting difference in a student's life.

Kids may or may not forget what you taught them, but they will <u>never</u> forget how you made them feel. If you aren't sold yet, try it out. But remember, you have to *mean* it.

180

Students or statistics?

"Statistics are no substitute for judgment."

- Henry Clay

Day after day, many teachers are pressured to focus on one thing, and one thing only — *student data*. Where are they showing growth? How are they performing? Are they ready for this year's standardized test? It can often feel like there is little time for anything that does not improve test scores. Teach, test, analyze scores, repeat. Teach, test, analyze scores, repeat. There is more pressure on school systems, more pressure on principals, more pressure on teachers, and more pressure on students. We've been in this era for over a decade now, and everyone is feeling the heat.

While we fully agree that the overarching goal of improving the rigor of education in America is a great step forward for our country, we also acknowledge that all the attention to academic progress has had an unforeseen side effect. Unfortunately, we are so intensely focused on curriculum and content mastery that we are in danger of forgetting about children. *We, with all the best intentions in the world, all too often forget that those statistics represent living, breathing kids.* Kids with a whole lot more on their minds than how their proficiency levels compare to respective children in other countries.

We don't mean to make standardized testing and student proficiency the enemy, we are simply trying to point out that we teach *real kids with real problems that need more from their teachers than content mastery.* Sadly, many students in need of encouragement look to their teachers, and find that their teachers are too distracted with the latest performance indicator to notice or offer help.

We owe it to our students to treat them as more than a number on the next school data report. We owe it to them and to our country to teach them that there is more to life than preparing for a standardized test. They need encouragement from teachers that will help guide them through difficult circumstances as well as curriculum standards. We need students to feel like their school cares about the days of their life that will occur *after* they take "the test." Again, academic growth, content mastery, and curriculum standards are *extremely important*, but let's not forget that there are some other things (that will never show up on a standardized test) that are pretty important too.

SUMMARY

Plastic tables, folding chairs, bad spaghetti, and store bought cookies, it was the quintessential church picnic. My wife and I (Rob) sat down and began making small talk with the girl sitting next to us. She was a senior in college and the conversation quickly drifted in a predictable direction: What's your name? What are you studying? She then returned the favor and asked me what I "do." When I told her that I teach eighth grade American history her eyes lit up: "Oh my goodness! My favorite teacher was my eighth grade history teacher! He was so awesome. I loved his class."

Curious, as any teacher would be, I asked her why her teacher was so special. She went on to explain that among the many things she liked about her teacher, he seemed to have a way to inspire her, to challenge her to be something bigger and better than she had expected for herself. She couldn't quite put her finger on it, but he had a way of making her believe she could be *more*.

Inspired, and wanting to know more about a teacher that could make a student light up eight years (and many teachers) later, I asked her where she went to school. When she answered, I think I dropped my fork into my spaghetti—she went to school where Scotty used to teach.

After a long silence I asked her, "Was your teacher by any chance named Mr. Hicks?" When she smiled, I knew the answer: "Yes."

Working with Scotty for the last several years has taught me a lot of things (to extend department deadlines, not to expect him to find anything on his desk, to hide my candy, to make extra copies, etc.), but above all else, he has challenged me to:

Be a teacher that spends a little more time on inspiration and a little less time on information.

I drove home from the picnic suspecting there weren't many college seniors describing my class in the same way. I'm sure I could find plenty of students who liked my class, thought I was funny, or considered me a "good teacher," but chances were high that I wouldn't find any that were inspired by their one hundred and eighty day venture in my classroom. I have tried, and in many regards am still trying, to reverse that trend.

Encouragement is one of the most powerful tools an educator can use to make a difference. Just the other day, my wife heard a mother call her six year old daughter "stupid" in front of a large group of people. What kind of message is being sent to that poor little girl? Where do you think *she* will be in twenty years? Kids *need* encouragement. Make your classroom a place they can find it!

Bad Apples?

Chapter 12

Recognizing what makes your students who they are

"If you can learn a simple trick, Scout, you'll get along a lot better with all kinds of folks. You never really understand a person until you consider things from his point of view, until you climb inside of his skin and walk around in it."

- Atticus Finch (To Kill a Mockingbird)

Understanding where kids are coming from is a lesson I (Rob) had to learn in a humiliating and heart-breaking way during my first year teaching. Like many new clueless teachers, I was more or less eaten alive my first semester. But, upon the recommendation of many trusted colleagues, I spent my first year focusing one hundred percent on classroom management. About February, my work started paying off. I was more adept at management, and my classroom was actually starting to run smoothly.

Determined not to lose any ground I had gained, I kept pressing in and expecting more and more respect from my students. One Monday, a girl who normally wasn't much trouble sat staring off into space. I noticed she was off task, and I called her to the carpet. No response. She stared straight through me. The class sat in silence anticipation — there was about to be a throw down, and they had front row seats. I insisted she do what I say and wouldn't take "no" for an answer. I called her out and she exploded on me — expletives and all. An administrator was called, she was escorted out, and given a three day suspension.

After school, I sat at my desk recalling the incident, and honestly, I was proud of myself. "If you are in Mr. Kuban's class, you do what Mr. Kuban says," I thought boastfully. Then, I heard a knock at the door. It was my assistant principal. She stopped by to get my side of the story. Nothing major. Then, *she dropped a bomb.* The student broke down in her office and explained her pent up rage: Her mom's new boyfriend moved in with them, and was prostituting my fourteen year old student for drug money.

My assistant principal left the room, and I put my head in my hands and cried. There was nothing else I could do but cry. *I was ashamed of myself* — a few minutes earlier I had my feet up on my desk declaring that there was a new sheriff in town — and all I did was make some poor girl going through hell on earth feel even worse about herself.

I drove home that afternoon and vowed to *never forget that day* — that I would always try to remember and recognize where my students were coming from. Even today, I constantly remind myself:

They almost always have a reason.

When students act like academics is the last thing on their minds, it's most likely because academics _is_ the last thing on their minds. Remind yourself when a student misbehaves or shifts in and out of focus: *They almost always have a reason.*

It's easy to be deceived into thinking that a story like the one above could never happen where you teach, but nothing could be further from the truth. My (Scotty) last teaching placement was not only a suburban school, but one of the most affluent areas in the entire district. In every sense of the word, my previous position was on the "right" side of the tracks; however, right there in the heart of upper-middle class America, I taught a student I will never forget.

She was a sweet, young girl with a gentle smile on her face as she walked into my classroom to begin eighth grade.

186

While most of her classmates spent the summer soaking up the sun at the family's beach house, she had a summer that, even thinking about it today, brings a sick feeling to my stomach. That summer, she was raped by her twenty-nine year old half brother after he was released from jail for other violent crimes. Immediately after the rape, another one of her half brothers (nineteen years old and also one of my former students) went to the accused rapist's apartment and killed him, stabbing him more than twenty times.

A couple months after being raped by her violent felon half brother that was then killed by her other half brother, *she walked into my classroom.* Somehow I was supposed to teach this girl about Native Americans, the Civil War, and everything in between. *How would she be able to focus on anything?* How could she actually think her schoolwork was important in her life? How could I ask her to do anything? I found that I had a deeper desire to pray for her than to teach her.

I still remember the first time she entered my classroom. Her mere presence at school was beyond an act of bravery. But to be honest, it was hard to tell her apart from the other students. She wore a smile and did her best to act as if she didn't have a single worry. If I hadn't known better, she would have blended in with every other student in the class...*she would have blended in with all the other students hiding behind smiles.*

While these two students certainly represent extreme cases, the reality is that *every* school in America has students with serious problems at home. Unfortunately, these kids often come with a label—the "Bad Apples" that will spoil the bunch. They are the ones that teachers in earlier grades give you a "head's up" on during in-service week when you receive your roster. It's easy to write them off before they even step foot in your room, but it's our job as teachers who want to make a difference to look past the labels.

Find the kid beneath the baggage.

At my previous school, I (Scotty) had a phone on my desk. This was back in the time when students were still passing notes instead of "stealth-texting" because none of them had their own personal mobile device. So students frequently needed to use my phone to call home. When basketball practice was canceled, lunch money was forgotten, a project was left at home, or any other such "emergency," my students would ask for permission to use my phone. This was permitted by the administration, but I decided to use it for something more—a way for distant teens to connect with their parents and say something they probably hadn't said in a while.

My policy was simple. If you wanted to use my phone, you must end the conversation by telling your parents: "I love you." If they were calling their parents, grandparents, or older siblings, the four-letter word had to be stated. If they didn't like the rule, there was a phone in the office. Some students complied without complaint, some whined, some ever so quietly mumbled those three words, and a few flat out refused and elected to use the office phone instead. While many parents commented on how much they loved the idea, I tell this story because of the time my policy ran into a student named Michael.

Despite being very mature for his age, Michael was one of the quiet kids that came with a label. The students called him "Goth" or "Emo," and his previous teachers had a few names for him as well. He only had a few outfits—all black—that he wore over, and over, and often smelled of body odor. He lived near the school and walked home where he lived with his mother. His father was in his life sporadically at best.

"Mr. Hicks, I need to call my dad. Can I use your phone?"

"Sure Michael, you know my policy. You just have to

tell him you love him before the conversation is over," I replied.

"Come on, Mr. Hicks. I don't want to walk down to the office."

"Well then, just tell him you love him."

At that he dropped his head and with determination in his voice said, "There is *no way* I will ever tell that man I love him, because I don't. *I hate him.*"

Over the years, I was always amazed at how many students had silly, childish reasons to try and get around my policy, but I knew that whatever emotion Michael was feeling wasn't an excuse—*it was real.* I am not sure why Michael hated his dad so much, but hearing the anger in his voice made me see something in Michael that I couldn't see before. I had to tweak my policy after that day. It made me remember—*they almost always have a reason.*

Some students come into your room with a chip on their shoulder and others come in desperate to sit alone in the corner. Either way, there are a lot of things troubling today's youth. To put it plainly, *our students are* not *growing up the way many of us did.*

Very few teachers are unaware of the *major* changes in the average American home front. According to recent studies, the number of students living in a single parent home has *drastically* increased over the last thirty years (and yes, it is usually single mothers carrying the load). Further still, many of the children that do have two parents at home often see their teachers more than parents because Mom and Dad are spending more time at work to pay the bills. This is not to say that families aren't trying to stay together, or that all parents are workaholics. We are simply trying to make the point that many families are struggling, for some reason or another, and no one is more affected by this than *the children.*

We can hide behind ignorance or apathy and assume that our students are growing up in the same world we did, but the evidence points to the contrary. The statistical likelihood of a student in your class struggling with a recent divorce, job loss, poverty, or an absent father is high to say the least (among countless other struggles as well). We aren't trying to point a finger at any section of society (every working, single mom deserves a medal!); instead, we are trying to expose the reality that students are carrying *a lot more* than we did growing up.

To make matters worse, many of these kids are turning to all the wrong places for acceptance and guidance. I (Scotty) certainly got into some trouble as a teen trying to find my place, but my mishaps were minor—more or less limited to the small town I grew up in. Today, kids can get into more trouble on their cell phone than I could have ever dreamed even existed as a teenager in Sweetwater, Tennessee. Many of the dejected and neglected kids today find their only escape in a digital world that exposes them to all kinds of evils at an unbelievably early age. Many of the places that children today run to as an answer to their depression, disinterest, or loneliness are leading them down dark paths.

How do you deal with this? How do you help a "Bad Apple" turn things around? It isn't easy, but the following section will look at a few ways to try to dodge the bruises.

Being fair isn't always...fair

I (Scotty) believe that the great majority of teachers try to be fair, but experience has taught me that sometimes educators go about "fairness" the wrong way. In an attempt to be as fair as possible, teachers create a zero tolerance attitude towards their students—a no "ifs, ands, and buts about it" mentality that holds *every* student to *exactly* the same standard *every* time.

In a way, I understand their approach. Every educator can relate to the seemingly endless list of excuses that fall upon our ears. Things like:

- "I didn't get the project done because my brother was using the computer to play fantasy football."
- "Oh, we had to do that? I thought you said it was *optional.*"
- "I did it, but I lost it."
- "I turned that in already!"
- "I was meeting with my parole officer."
- "I had to get my nails done."
- "I know you assigned it three weeks ago, but our computer quit working *last night.*"
- "I think the cleaning lady threw away my homework."
- "My mom told me I could turn it in late."
- "I wasn't tardy, my backpack was here."

When you hear things like this day in and day out, you can easily become jaded and think that students *never* have a legitimate excuse. *But what if they do?*

How do you balance a desire to be fair with the fact that kids often have legitimate reasons for not making your class priority one? If we are honest, we will admit that:

"Fairness" is relative.

It certainly *sounds* fair to treat everyone exactly the same, but in reality, it is not. Consider the young girl I taught that was raped by her half brother only to have her other half brother avenge the act with murder. What exactly am I supposed to do as her teacher? *Should I have treated her like everyone else?* Wouldn't that be the "fair" thing to do? I think we can all agree that she didn't need a very clear understanding of the three branches of government during this difficult season of life. What she needed was compassion, love, and understanding.

What about students who receive their only real meal at school? What about students who live in a situation where school is the only place they actually feel safe? What about students who don't bust the door down when school lets out because home is the last place they want to go?

In light of this, we believe that *students will be most successful when they trust that their teacher understands where they are coming from.* It can be hard to distinguish real excuses from fake ones (well okay, sometimes it's pretty easy!), but often we are left riding the fine line between accountability and reality. You could buy a polygraph machine or you could simply:

Create an environment where excuses don't matter.

Forgot to turn something in? Fine, turn it in late with an appropriate penalty. Fail a test? Fine, do a re-teaching assignment and take it or a similar version again. *Allow students to survive your class even when life isn't going perfectly.* Simple as that—just allow students the opportunity to recover if, for some reason or another, they have fallen behind. Give them permission to have a bad day, slip up, or have space to process the hardships they may be experiencing at home.

Some teachers would argue that such a philosophy is soft and teaches students that they can be lazy. These teachers tend to argue that their zero tolerance philosophy is teaching students priceless "life lessons." *But is it really?* It may sound good to preach that such a strategy is teaching students all about life in the real world, but is it working? *Are teaching and learning really happening in the process?* In other words, when a slacking student is exposed to a life lesson, do they *learn* the lesson? Do they change? Do they suddenly realize: "Oh man, I can't believe I failed that test! I was being lazy, and it caught up to me. Someday life will not be nearly as forgiving, so I need to make sure to study

192

more for the next test." No, most of these students fail repeatedly, proving that nothing—no life lessons <u>and</u> no content—was actually learned. In all honesty, this philosophy, though it looks good on paper, doesn't hold a lot of water. The testimonies of *actual* success are few and far between.

There are countless troubles in the lives of the students who sit before us every day (even those that seem like everything is fine on the surface). If our approach to these students is to hold them to absolute, non-negotiable standards, we will *never* reach them. Ironically, *we do this to prepare them for the theoretical real world off in the distant future, but completely ignore the actual real world awaiting them outside of school.* Students will be best prepared for life if they have teachers that meet them where they are, encourage them, believe in them, and give them more than one opportunity to be successful.

Certainly, a few teachers are thinking: "But what if they <u>*deserve*</u> that grade?" And they may. This is a gray area that requires professional judgment. If you are teaching an Advanced Placement High School Honors class and a few students are slacking, then by all means, hold them to the expected standards of an Honors class. However, if you are like the majority of teachers out there with a mixed group of kids coming from all walks of life, then take time to reflect over what *fairness* really means in your classroom. Just remember: A lot of these students probably *deserve* some *other* things they aren't getting as well—like supportive parents, a stable home, or food on the table. *They almost always have a reason.*

Feel free to disagree, but *we have taught too many students going through hell at home to worry about whether an assignment is turned in late.* If you aren't quite sure what to make of all of this, go ahead and give it try (in an appropriate way for your classroom). What you'll find is the students with legitimate excuses will typically catch back up, and the ones with fake excuses will never give you anything but more excuses! Another chance gives those lugging baggage some much needed compassion, and as for the slackers attempting to take advantage of the system, they always find a way to fail with the same surprising efficiency. *When you are uncertain what to do, always give a student the benefit of the doubt.*

Take a step back from your classroom and you'll realize that your students, regardless of where you teach, are dealing with a lot more than you think. Meeting kids where they are is worth the effort for an educator seeking to make a positive impact. After all, if we are humble enough to live out the advice of Atticus Finch, we might realize that *maybe* <u>we</u> *aren't as different from our students as we think...*

Throwing stones?

Students are not the only ones making excuses. *How many times have you been guilty of the exact same things that you criticize in your classroom?* We like to think that we never commit the same egregious errors of our student populations, but maybe, as the old saying goes: "Those in glass houses shouldn't throw stones."

Classroom: *"How can you not have paper and something to write with for the fourth time this week?!? It is only Tuesday!"*
Faculty meeting: *"Excuse me, can I borrow your pen for a second? Yeah, a piece of paper too."*

Classroom: [After a One Direction ring tone pierces through your lesson] *"Bring me the cell phone now. You know the rules. It should have been turned off."*
Faculty meeting: [After an AC/DC ring tone interrupts your principal's speech] *"Sorry, I thought it was muted."*

Classroom: *"How could you be twenty seconds late AGAIN!"*
Teacher: *"Oh no! I am late to bus duty AGAIN!"*

Student in a classroom: *"Why do we have to know this? How is this going to help me in life?"*
Teacher in professional development session: *"Why do we have to know this? How is this going to help me in my classroom?"*

We aren't pointing fingers, just reminding you that those of us in the so called "real world" are just as prone to forgetfulness, laziness, unpreparedness...and just about everything else we accuse our students of doing! In light of this, we ought to show *a little* more patience when our students—who are still children—show some of the bad habits that we as adults have yet to conquer.

Reach them to teach them

Many of our students are alone, fatherless, impoverished, depressed, neglected, or unspeakably worse; and half the time all we appear to care about is whether or not they have completed some worksheet. A colleague and good friend of mine (Scotty), Amy Crawford started an organization called *Reach Them to Teach Them* to remind and inspire teachers and others that *we must first reach a child's heart before we can teach their minds.* All teachers need that reminder, and we need it often. The first step in reaching a student's heart is getting to know who they are and where they are coming from.

We shouldn't expect students to "get over" their problems, we should teach them to <u>overcome</u> their problems.

The only way a student will learn to overcome problems at home is to learn how to navigate adversity at school (rather

195

than school being just another troubling environment). Teachers who *reach and teach* their kids can be an irreplaceable source of consistent guidance, encouragement, *and understanding.*

In an earlier chapter, I (Rob) mentioned that some of the most resilient and inspirational students I have *ever* taught came from my inner city placement. I had the privilege of teaching kids who had every reason to give up and give in, but had the courage and perseverance to set their life on a different course. *In almost every case,* these students pointed to a handful of <u>teachers</u> that met them where they were and offered guidance, encouragement, and support.

I (Scotty) am happy to report that the young lady from my eighth grade class who experienced overwhelming tragedy not only graduated from high school but is now attending college. This is undoubtedly due to her courageous and determined heart, but I would also like to believe that it is due to teachers and other adults who had enough understanding and concern to focus on what truly mattered in her life...*which wasn't always her grades.*

From bad apples to bullets

Why go to such great lengths to reach students? Why go above and beyond the call of duty to connect with a child that doesn't fit in? Why trouble yourself with a student who seems to be nothing but trouble? Sadly, we live in a time when many struggling students have resorted to violent measures in a grim attempt to deal with their problems. Unfortunately, the idea of a "survival guide" for teachers isn't just limited to finding your way through curriculum or classroom management. In recent years, teacher survival has taken on a literal meaning. As we all know, shooting after shooting has begun to deteriorate the overall sense of security and safety in America. It seems that no place, not even school, is sacred anymore. It is with great sorrow that we even have to discuss this topic, but we *must.*

First and foremost, *we want to recognize and honor those who have given their lives in defense of children in schools across America.* They are heroes whose names we may never know. We also want to recognize and honor all who choose to stay in this field despite what is being broadcasted on the news. It takes a certain amount of courage to do what we do — to stand up and stay put — and we don't want that to be overlooked.

Society continues to debate placing resource officers in every school, arming teachers, locking down the facilities, and tightening gun control. Such defensive measures may improve security, but meanwhile, there are things *you* <u>can</u> and <u>should</u> do now.

Your students depend on <u>you</u> for their safety.

Do everything in your power to ensure your school is safe. It could be as simple as:

- Making sure doors are locked.
- Requiring visitors to enter securely through the front office.
- Questioning every unrecognizable person you pass in the halls (even though nine hundred and ninety nine times out of a thousand they are probably a legitimate visitor).
- Investigating anything suspicious.
- Being very aware of the emergency procedures.

Security and preventative measures such as these are very important and will help protect a school, but to make our schools *and* our society as safe as possible, we must go one step further.

In all of the heated debate revolving around how to prevent such incidents, many neglect to address the root of the problem—the question of "why?" *Why* are these gunmen shooting up schools, shopping malls, movie theaters, and college campuses? What leads a person to this point? It's easy to point the finger at some form of "mental instability" (which passes the buck and passively argues that such events are not really preventable), but it is much more than that. People who murder others in a random act of violence rarely do so because of mere mental instability or one single event that occurred in their life. They usually do so because they slowly lost hope in a world that no longer makes sense to them. *Once hope is gone, all hell breaks loose.*

As an educator, you can only do so much to prevent some stranger from sneaking on campus and going on a shooting rampage, *but you can do a great deal in preventing your students from becoming that stranger.* Reach out to all of your students—*especially* the ones with a label—and let them know that you believe in them even if no one else does.

Do everything you can to give a kid hope that has none.

It may not change a thing, but then again it might. *Many kids are drowning in despair, and you could be the one to give them hope.*

You have nothing to lose and everything to gain by trying to reach *every* student. In fact, we are certain that dozens of shootings *never* happened because a teacher reached a troubled youth. You won't read about these in the papers or watch the aftermath on the news, *but it happens.* Society is made safer every day because teachers, teachers like you, make it safer by touching the lives of troubled kids.

That student who keeps talking to you as if you are his only friend in the building, that girl who just looks angry all the time, that boy who doesn't have a prayer, that girl who gave up on hope long ago—reach them. Be the hero that no one knows about—*reach all of them.*

SUMMARY

Students come from all backgrounds: poor, wealthy, neglected, smothered, loved, and hated. We never know what might be hiding behind that timid face on the first day of school, but we do know that everyone of them needs love, discipline, guidance, and a sound education. It is our job to make sure they receive it.

Fortunately, students' backgrounds don't always determine their future. Teachers can focus on "the way it should be" (or the way it used to be), or they can focus on the kids who desperately need them *now*. You can't do anything about their past, but you certainly <u>can</u> affect their future.

From Bad Days to
Burning Out to Being Real

Chapter 13

Teaching when "real life" gets in the way

"The best thing about the future is that it only comes one day at a time."

- Abraham Lincoln

It was the last Saturday before starting a new school year, and I (Rob) was sawing boards on my table saw. Nothing out of the ordinary. I'm sure I was keeping the neighbors awake at 10:00 pm, but I was determined to finish my project that night. Sawdust was flying, and my pace steadily quickened as the night got later.

I heard something behind me and as I turned, my right arm swung at my side and gracefully glanced the *still raging saw blade!* I screamed at the top of my lungs and started frantically looking for the end of my thumb. Suddenly, I realized it was attached by a few lucky skin cells that escaped the wrath of the blade. I rushed inside and yelled up the stairs: "We have to go the hospital!" My wife came running down, and in a matter of minutes our kids were at the neighbors, and we were off to the emergency room with my hand — *and what was left of my thumb* — in a bowl of ice.

They "temporarily" re-attached my thumb and wrote me a prescription for enough painkillers to knock out an elephant. Someone working the graveyard shift wrapped up my hand, and we headed home. *Thirty hours later I am standing in the cafeteria welcoming students on the first day of school!* I was a sight to see — walking around with my arm raised high to alleviate throbbing and my mummified hand looking as if it was bandaged by a ten year old boy scout. Throw in a few hundred milligrams of serious painkillers coursing through my veins, and needless to say, I made *quite* an impression on my new students.

To be honest, I have no idea what I said—or what I did—those first couple days of school (though *several* parents informed me at open house that I was the topic of their dinner conversation that night).

I learned two valuable lessons from that experience. First, keep the blade guard on your table saw—it's there for a reason. But more importantly, I learned that *sometimes life just happens*.

Sooner or later, life <u>will</u> get in the way of your classroom.

The story above is humorous to read, but the honest truth is that when life gets interrupted, it usually isn't funny at all (I can promise you that I was not laughing that night in the ER!).

Bad days

"Call me as soon as you can. It is an emergency." - Dad

I (Rob) had never received a message like that before. Obviously something was wrong, *very* wrong. My heart pounded as I took a few steps away from my students and called my dad. We talked for a few minutes and he informed me that after several tests, his doctor had found a growth on his pancreas...and they thought it was cancer. There are a lot more questions than answers at the beginning—as anyone who has battled cancer knows—and my mind was beginning to spin out of control.

I wanted to see my dad, be with my wife, and hug my son, *but I couldn't*. Why not? You guessed it—I had to teach two more classes before I could go home that day. And as it turned out, I had to teach two more school years before my dad could go *home*. With godliness, courage, and integrity, my dad fought and lost, a two year battle against cancer. In the middle of this very difficult and trying season of life, our daughter was born with a rare brain disorder. Any attempts I had made up until this point to keep myself together were shattered. *Nothing would ever be the same.*

While I was juggling the painful process of my dad's cancer and my precious new daughter's physical therapy, occupational therapy, speech therapy, developmental coaching, and neurology appointments, guess what else was going on? *Eighth grade American History.* Unfortunately, my classes and students didn't stay on hold until my life stabilized. Some days were better than others, but I didn't have the slightest clue how to make it through the mess I was in.

We could go on and on with stories like these. Scotty could tell you about the day he was brought to the office during class to answer a phone call from his Platoon Sergeant who called to inform him that in a few months he would be heading to war (and the following call he had to make to his pregnant wife to let her know that he was getting shipped off to battle). He could also tell you about the Sunday night he stood by his father's bedside in the hospital trying to understand why the doctor was suggesting they give his dad a healthy dose of morphine and cut off life support.

Every teacher will inevitably face the daunting task of teaching class in the middle of major life struggles. From financial struggles to deaths in the family to trying to pull off a lesson nine months into pregnancy, teachers still have to teach. Regardless of how *Murphy's Law* finds its way into your life, you must still stand up in front of class and do your job. This is one of the most difficult aspects of our career—you can't hide behind a desk, a closed door, or voicemail. You are on public display for seven hours a day, five days a week. If you work in an office and life is crumbling around you, your co-workers will understand and act accordingly. They will give you space and try to be encouraging. *Not so with students.* Inquisitive kids with poor judgment and timing often surround us while we struggle to keep it together until the final bell, only to start over again the next morning. How do you do it? We have been through a good deal of challenging seasons in our tenure as teachers, and we hope the following thoughts serve you well the next time trouble comes knocking on your door.

Don't

Lie to your students (and yourself). The first temptation is to bottle it all up, never take a day off, never skip a beat, pretend like life is peachy keen, and hope that you can convince your students and yourself that there is nothing but sunshine and rainbows on the horizon. *This doesn't work because it isn't real.* You can't click your heels three times and escape. It isn't healthy or practical, and will eventually catch up to you. Emotions this powerful either get pushed down so deep they can only escape through a catastrophic meltdown of epic proportions (potentially during class), or worse, they will die altogether. You will ultimately sever that part of your heart if you attempt to stay numb to your feelings for too long.

Break down in front of your students. The second temptation is to do the opposite and unload every ounce of baggage, hurt, and pain in every class. The classroom is not a place to vent pent up frustration, and students are not adolescent shrinks trained to analyze your issues. Having an emotional break down in front of your students can create a lot more problems than the temporary relief the anger or tears may bring in the moment. If you feel your emotions rising to the surface, step outside the classroom (if possible), and take a moment to regain your composure. Pray, take a deep breath, visualize your happy place, whatever method works for you. *Neither you nor your students will benefit when you consistently try to teach on the verge of an emotional breakdown.*

Do

Strive for a balance between the extremes above. Allow yourself to have some bad days and some lackluster lessons. When I (Rob) was walking through worlds of struggle with my dad and daughter, I passed out more worksheets, showed more videos, and spent more time at my desk (and even had a few parents complain because of it). I know that may sound unpolished and unprofessional, but I needed some space to process and mature during such a difficult season. It was *extremely hard*, and I wished I could have just taken two years off, but bills had to be paid and lessons had to be taught. Also, I would be lying if I told you I held it all together. There were moments, such as the time a student shared a weekend story about doing something fun with his dad, where my emotions made it to the surface. On these occasions, I was always surprised by how patient, understanding, and encouraging my students were. *Great teachers won't make their personal life part of their curriculum or use their struggles to excuse poor performance, but they won't expect life to leave them alone one hundred and eighty days a year either.*

Learning how to walk through these difficult periods can make or break your career. Not only that, it may just make or break you as a person. As the old adage states: "Adversity is a great teacher." *Let it teach you.* Sooner or later, life will regain a sense of normalcy. By God's grace, my dad has gone home to heaven and my daughter's progress is nothing short of a miracle, but looking back I can see how the challenges I had to face have made me a better person, a better man, a better husband, and a better father. In a lot of ways, they have also made me a better teacher. Despite the external hardships you may be facing, it is essential to greet students with an encouraging smile, be the leader in the room, and *teach* your students. This isn't easy and most of us will perform miserably at the attempt, but it is worth the effort. *Why?* Well, students *still* need to grow academically, but something much deeper and more significant is going on during this process than mere academics.

After going from teaching to active duty in Iraq and then immediately back to teaching, I (Scotty) struggled immensely in the classroom. It was almost like a dream. One minute I am in an armored Humvee escorting high ranking officers through a combat zone, the next minute I am escorting students to an assembly. One minute I am holding an M-16 and yelling the few Arabic words I knew to an escalating crowd of Iraqi citizens, the next minute I am holding a dry erase marker teaching the effects of the Civil War to a class of thirteen-year olds. One minute I'm sitting at a funeral of a father of four killed by an I.E.D., the next minute I'm sitting in a parent conference reviewing an I.E.P.

Needless to say, upon my return, I had some serious difficulties in the classroom. After serving eight months of active duty, I only had a month off before having to teach the last nine weeks of school. *My heart was elsewhere.* Burdened with the guilt of leaving many of my brothers in arms fighting without me and still reflecting on the images of war, my thoughts dwelled on *everything* but lesson plans and academic growth. As if the adjustment from active duty weren't enough to sap my strength, I had just become a new dad. My son, Lincoln, was born two weeks after I left for active duty, and my return home not only meant adjusting to being a civilian—I also had to adjust to being a daddy to an eight month old baby! Again, one minute I am cleaning sand out of my M-16, the next minute I am cleaning the aftermath of sweet potatoes and green beans off of baby Lincoln's behind! I was going through the motions of being a teacher but felt certain that I wasn't making a positive impact on my students.

Six years later, I was contacted by a former student who was then majoring in history with the hopes of becoming a teacher. Through his college education program, he needed to conduct a classroom observation and asked if he could observe me. I didn't remember much about the young man, except that he had to have brain surgery that year and the projections for his future were questionable. I tried my best to encourage him for the few weeks I taught him before his surgery, but I was wrestling through the new responsibilities of parenting and re-adjusting to civilian life and felt like I had little, if anything, to offer. Yet, six years later, there he stood healthy and strong (playing college baseball as a matter of fact), telling me that *I* was one of the reasons he was becoming a teacher. *I couldn't believe it.*

I say all of this not to pretend like I am an amazing teacher that can change the lives of my students even during my darkest days (the rest of my students that year probably have forgotten my name). My point is that we *always* have the power to make an impact, and often when we least expect it. I have come to realize that the challenges I experienced changed me as a person, helped me to mature, and made me the sort of person that an 8th grader awaiting brain surgery could connect with—could trust. Though I didn't realize it at the time, he appreciated the fact that I was doing my best to overcome the difficulties I was facing, and it gave him strength to do the same.

We too often forget that we have students showing up and fighting just as hard (if not harder) than we are to make it through another day because of what they are dealing with in their own lives. Not all of them were up late waiting in line for the latest *Hunger Games* premier or playing *X-Box* til the wee hours of the morning with their friends. Many of them are fighting illness of their own, dealing with the loss of a loved one, coping with poverty, caught in the middle of an ugly divorce, or worse. A word of encouragement or a sense of stability and strength may be just what your students need at that moment in *their* lives. They lack the maturity to make it through many of their own hardships. You can be a "safe zone" where everything is stable and secure. They may need advice, and they may just simply need *you*.

It's yet another part of being a teacher that no one was trained for—where no one knows quite what to do or say when students drag the skeletons out of their closet during planning period. You may feel the need to send them to guidance and you may choose to handle it yourself, but the fact remains that for many students school is the most stable support structure in their lives. Even in your own difficult times, those students *still need you*. The year my (Rob) dad was dying of cancer, I had two students whose father was fighting cancer as well. I wrote them a letter and talked with them a time or two, but honestly have no idea if I made a difference. Either way, *I'm glad I tried*. I'm glad I didn't keep a "professional distance" and leave two scared thirteen-year-olds trying to figure things out on their own.

Deal with your problems as best as you can, but *remember that you are not the only one with problems*. Teachers aren't the only ones that have bad days. You know from experience that strenuous seasons come and go, but chances are high that just about *every day you teach* at least one of your students is going through something difficult in their world. Pain does not discriminate by age and often hurts more when no one seems to notice. In light of this, do your best to make *every* day count. This is hard, especially when you are going through something yourself, but life doesn't stop for anyone—students or teachers alike. *Whatever you are facing, whatever your students are facing, make today count.*

Teaching through the drama of life may be one of the most difficult things we have to do as teachers, but when you can survive adversity with courage and maturity and help your students do the same, you open a door to transform lives for good. *After all, isn't this part of why we all became teachers in the first place?*

Speaking of why we all became teachers...let's take a moment to talk about how we all have considered becoming something *other than* a teacher!

Burning out

"Take this job and shove it. I ain't workin' here no more."
- Johnny Paycheck

Hopefully none of us have been quite as passionate about quitting as Mr. Paycheck, but the honest truth is that a great majority of teachers have seriously thought about leaving the profession (for one reason or another). We know we don't have to tell you this, but *teaching is tough.* Though it may be difficult to convince others of this fact, *we* know it to be true.

The task of teaching a class full of kids is stressful enough by itself; however, when you add the stresses of life, evaluations, constantly changing expectations, ever evolving curriculum, unsupportive parents, cynical colleagues, piles of paperwork, duties outside of the classroom, little respect from society, a much smaller paycheck than other professionals, TESTS, TESTS, and more TESTS, the job quickly loses its luster. Many of us may have started out like a sparkler on the fourth of July, brightening the world everywhere we went, but as we all know...*sparklers eventually burn out.* If you can relate to this analogy, you are not alone.

Every teacher that stays in it long enough goes through some level of burn out.

There is something comforting and uniting to know that all of us experience burn out during our careers.

About five years into teaching, I (Scotty) went through a pretty severe season of burn out. I appeared to have the perfect placement—teaching in a great school in a great community. I had a five-minute commute, supportive parents, and some of the top performing students in the state. My standardized test scores were exceptionally high, and my lessons and assessments were already put together because I taught *one* subject all day each year. I was living the dream. I had every reason to be happy…*but I wasn't.*

My fire had turned to fading embers. Five years in and I had all but lost my love of teaching. Everyone, *especially* my students, took notice. My classes were becoming more and more disruptive, and I was growing less and less committed.

Now that I am looking back—and blessed with the wisdom that hindsight brings—I can see many reasons why I nearly drowned in discontent. First off, I had very few real connections to other faculty members. Not to say we all need to work with our best friend, but in some ways, I was a lone wolf. Don't get me wrong, I worked with a *great* group of teachers whom I respected, but they were all female. Everyday, I ate lunch with fifteen women and though most I'd consider as close friends, I can't recall a single discussion involving football, cage fighting, cars, or much of anything that truly interested me. In all honesty, the estrogen levels were just a little too high for an old country boy from Sweetwater, Tennessee like myself. Gender differences aside, I was on the verge of burn out because I *felt alone.*

It also didn't help that many of my non-teacher friends, with less education, were making a lot more money. In fact, money *was* an issue—*a big one.* My wife and I agreed that she needed to stay home and take care of our babies, but money was tight with two kids and one paycheck…*especially* when it's a teacher's paycheck! To cover the bills, I took a second job on nights and weekends and easily logged sixty plus hours a week (sometimes a lot closer to eighty than sixty!). I didn't have the luxury of worrying about whether or not my classroom exhibited innovative and effective instruction—I had to worry about my home exhibiting electricity. After subsisting like this for a few years, my confidence that a career in education was the best means to support my family was disappearing faster than my last paycheck.

I was seriously considering leaving the profession altogether when by happenstance I met a teacher from a surrounding district. He had left the system in which I was currently teaching, and claimed it was one of the best decisions he had ever made. I knew neighboring school systems paid more, but didn't think it would be worth the drive. He convinced me otherwise.

I soon discovered that the difference in pay (including benefits) was nearly twenty-five percent more, so gas money was no longer a concern. I began sending out resumes and within two years landed a position teaching the exact same grade and subject at a great school making much more money. In fact, the pay increase I received at my new position (with a track coaching stipend) allowed me to quit my second job. I quickly made some close friends on the staff, found some guys to talk to about cars and cage fighting, and I honestly couldn't be happier.

I know what you may be thinking: "Good for you—but what about those of us that can't shuffle school systems and teach the same thing for a twenty five percent raise? What are *we* supposed to do?" The answer isn't always relocation. That is only a portion of my story. In fact, I can look back and see several other things that I did (or didn't do) that contributed to the extinguishing of my educational flame. *In a lot of ways, my journey through burn out was mostly my own fault.* I took no preventative measures and then, when dread started to sink in, I had no clue how to overcome it.

This is an area that every teacher must take seriously. Some professions drain you physically, some mentally, and some emotionally. Teaching is a perfect storm—possessing the ability to drain you in every manner possible (about the only thing that doesn't seem to get drained during a school day is your bladder!). Your job is physically exhausting, mentally fatiguing, and emotionally taxing. By the time the last bell rings, every last ounce of anything you had to offer is depleted. With this kind of job description, *some level of burn out is inevitable.* If you haven't experienced burn out, just wait—it's coming. If you have, you know how brutal and widespread it can be on everything from your classroom to your family to your social life.

Because of this spiraling effect, you must choose to be proactive—to stay ahead of the curve—and remember to take care of yourself. We have already addressed many ways to avoid burn out: keeping a sense of humor, focusing on what you do best, maintaining effective classroom management, improving time management, having a life outside of school, getting adequate rest, staying organized, and keeping your classroom creative. All of these suggestions will definitely help you to maintain your spark, *but we all know that these strategies are not enough.* To win the battle against burn out (preventing _and_ overcoming it), you must do *more*...or perhaps you may need to do *less.*

Pace your passion. Many teachers are misled into believing that the best thing you can do for your career, your students, and your school is to pour every bit of your being into education. This isn't healthy. You will not last. *You can't allow your classroom to choke out every other area of your life.* This might temporarily appear to alleviate burn out because your classes are going well, but devoting all (or the overwhelming majority) of your energy to your classes will eventually backfire and lead to a bitter end.

Pursue other passions. Re-read our chapter titled: *Get a Life!* You must have a life *outside* of school to be the best you can be *inside* of school. Remember to do things you enjoy as often as you can. Whether that means bike riding, barbequing, or listening to bluegrass, refuel with good times and *add* energy to your tank. *Put down the papers and do something un-educational.*

Make friends at work. Find some guys, gals, or a combination of the two that make for good conversation (and *no*, talking about teaching doesn't count!). Much like my (Scotty) own experience, *you are more likely to get burned out if you feel alone.* The best way to prevent this is to make friends with your co-workers. If you do so, then you are surrounded by people that will make you laugh when you need to smile or encourage you when you are down. Don't be a hermit that hides in your room. This will leave you stranded and secluded in seasons when you need support.

Love your lunch. Teachers must guard the few sacred minutes we have to step out of our classroom and interact with adults. Right in the middle of the day (unless you work in an elementary school and eat lunch at 10:00AM!), you have a "half time" to regroup and recharge. Use it to unwind, let loose, and connect with your friends in the building. Spending those precious moments grading papers, sitting alone in your room, or talking with other teachers about the stresses of teaching robs you of the energizing effect lunch can have. *If you think it is a waste of time to spend lunch shooting the breeze, then you are shooting yourself in the foot.*

Take as many vacations as possible. It's no secret that one of the biggest perks to teaching is the time off. Use it! Go on trips, sleep in, and get out of the house (talk to some seasoned teachers and you'll get some great tips on how to vacation inexpensively). *To make it in this profession, you have to realize the importance of using your time off to recharge your batteries.* You will certainly have to use some of your vacation time catching up on house projects or holiday decorating, but do your best to make sure you get to the end of a break *feeling* like you just had a break.

Exercise. While it may seem like strange advice, regular exercise will work wonders for your stamina. *Being healthy simply makes you feel better in every area of your life.* Walk, run, mow the yard, play with your kids—do whatever it takes to stay active, and you will find yourself less drained at the end of each school day.

Find a healthy release. We've said a lot about the stresses of education in this chapter. Well, all that stress has to go somewhere. *Find a healthy way to "de-stress."* Whether that means running, knitting, strumming a six string, reading fiction novels, or getting your nails done, find a way to zone out and let some of the day's stresses slide off your back. If you don't take the time to do this, your stress <u>will</u> find its way to the surface...usually in an unpleasant manner (just ask your friends and family).

Steal, pillage, and plunder. One major cause of burn out is trying to do everything yourself. Chances are you don't have to go more than a few classrooms down the hall to find great teaching ideas and materials. *Try to lessen the burden of responsibilities by collaborating with other teachers as often as you can.* When teachers work together, everyone gets to leave a little earlier. Be willing to borrow and share—whatever it takes to keep from re-inventing the wheel every day of every school year.

Invest in inspirational professional development. In many cases, I (Scotty) have found that *reading a good book on* *teaching or going to a high quality workshop helps to re-ignite my dwindling flame.* Know that every now and then, you will need to throw another log on the fire.

Don't dread <u>that</u> class. It seems that many teachers have *that* class—the one where the stars aligned and created a cataclysmic line up of "the usual suspects" that seem ten minutes away from bringing about the downfall of western civilization! Every teacher has taught this class. When you find yourself having a class roster that could easily be confused with a most wanted list and creating a seating chart feels like some strange and sinister form of a Sudoku puzzle, *focus on it as a challenge to fine tune your teaching skills instead of a pain that must be endured.* I (Rob) know that sounds impossible, but I found out early in my career that dreading a difficult class is often far more draining than actually teaching it. Not that teaching it is easy, but don't waste planning periods and nights lying in bed groaning over it—that will only make things worse. Experiment with that class to find new ways to engage difficult students. Doing so will pay dividends throughout the remainder of your career. If this describes the group of kids you have *all* day *every* day, start looking for some realistic classroom management solutions (and consider bribing the Guidance office next year...just kidding).

Make more money. Sure—easier said than done. We all know we didn't getting into teaching for the money, but now that we've got a mortgage, a family, a car payment, and student loans, we wouldn't mind a little more of it. To lessen financial stress, you have two options: Increase your income or decrease your lifestyle. Not that we picture a lot of teachers in Italian suits eating caviar at fine restaurants, but making *conservative* financial choices (such as when purchasing a home, vehicle, or even where and when to eat out) can minimize a lot of financial stress in your life.

Secondly, try to find ways to increase your income that do not add tremendous amounts of new stress. This could mean looking for a job in another school system or pursuing an administrative position; however, for most it will look more like obtaining a higher degree, tutoring, taking on extra paid duties, teaching summer school, or coaching. I (Rob) have found that I much prefer to supplement my income in ways that have nothing to do with my teaching position (I find this helps keep my "teaching stress" at a lower level). Either way, *minimizing expenses and increasing income will lessen one of teaching's greatest stresses.*

No child left behind? Any elementary teacher can tell you that an exceptionally high percentage of young boys think they are going to become professional athletes when they grow up. However, by the time these future superstars reach high school, many of them are benchwarmers at best. It appears that coaches do not adhere to leaving *"no athlete behind."* This is just one of countless examples proving that the pressure put on teachers regarding the overall success of every single student in every single skill set is...*unrealistic* (to put it politely).

It is common for teachers to wrestle with guilt when they stare into a sea of students and realize that some of them are destined for bad decisions, failure, or the nightly news. I (Scotty) used to get a little depressed thinking about the likely future of some my struggling students. It would often make me feel like I was responsible: Why can't I reach him? Why is she still failing when I have given her so many opportunities to pass? *Unfortunately, the pressure to turn every single student into an academic superstar has left many teachers discouraged and doubting their abilities.* Expectations of educational perfection have left many of us burned out, bitter, and feeling like failures ourselves. This stretch of wilderness has taken down *a lot* of teachers.

It is sad and tragic, but many students have a great deal

of external circumstances influencing their lives in a negative direction. Hopefully, your guidance and the advice of other caring individuals will sink in and give them a vision of a better future, but many times it will not. *Don't let this destroy your desire to make a difference.* Instead choose to focus on and celebrate the ones you <u>do</u> reach. Remember, *the best you can do is <u>all</u> you can do.*

Change. One of the main causes of burn out is feeling stuck. Grinding out each day until summer vacation is a terrible way to spend your career. *As the old saying goes: "Change is good."* Some change can help you re-ignite your spark. At the beginning of my (Scotty) career, I would have bet a million dollars that I would be teaching at my first school forever. I really didn't think things could be any better...but I was wrong. A moderate change in my career made a big difference in my attitude. You may not need to change school systems, but shifting the subject or grade level you teach may be enough to pull you out of your slump.

It's inevitable: As a teacher, you *will* stagger into the ring with burn out at various times in your career, and it is ultimately up to you to get out of it and make it to the next round — not just for your own sake but also for that of your school, colleagues, *and* students. Burning out is usually caused by an accumulation of separate issues, so when you start to smolder, investigate the specific issues and attitudes that cause you to lose steam and decide how to take action against them. It's okay to go through some down periods in your career, but it is not okay to stay down.

An apathetic teacher is a pathetic teacher.

If you want to have a successful *long-term* career as an educator, you have to remember to take care of *yourself.* Life is too short to be miserable, and if you are miserable, *so is*

217

everyone around you. There has never been, nor will there ever be, an unhappy yet successful teacher. Burn out is a lot like body odor—everyone breathes easier when you get it under control!

Being real

I (Scotty) once had a friend who had been dating a girl for quite a while when he finally decided it was time to get married. His girlfriend said yes to his proposal, and they set a date a few months later. I noticed that they argued a lot *before* they decided to get married, but couldn't believe how much strife and stress surrounded their engagement. Their whole wedding planning process had more drama than a "House Wives" reality show. When I tried to talk to him about it, he blamed it all on the fact that they both were in school and struggling financially. He claimed that once they graduated, got married, and combined their incomes, there would be, and I quote, "nothing left to argue about." Don't you love how much engaged couples know about marriage (kind of reminds you of how much you *thought* you knew about teaching before you actually taught)!?!

I wish I could say they lived happily ever after, but as you might have guessed, after they graduated, got married, and combined their incomes, they *still* managed to find things to argue about. Two short years after they tied the knot—they untied it. No one who watched them interact as a dating couple would have recommended they get married, but as we all know, relationships are complicated. They were sure they had found "the one" and no amount of reason, logic, or evidence could convince them otherwise.

Teaching is not too different. There are certainly a fair number of teachers out there that fell in love at first sight with summers off, snow days, and a 3:30 quitting time. *How hard could it be?* They probably heard about the challenges that came with the career, but like a person in a bad relationship, they chose to ignore them. Now they are married to the job, have a college degree and several years of their life invested in a career they hate.

Unfortunately, many teachers enter the profession with unrealistic expectations and often refuse to let go of them. We have chosen a very challenging and demanding career — and for those of you still wondering, *teaching will never be easy.* Even in the best situations teaching is still a very stressful job. Our profession is becoming more difficult as the years go by, and most likely, we will never feel fairly compensated for what we do day in and day out.

It is a calling not a career, only to be embraced by those who were destined for it. To make it in this field you have to be *realistic* — and accept your calling for better or worse, for richer or poorer (most likely poorer!).

All teachers have to frequently remind themselves why they became a teacher.

You may have gotten into it for what you could get for yourself, but if you stay in that mindset you will end up miserable. You just won't find society, your students, or your bank account bending over backwards to say "thank you." In many ways, teaching really is like marriage: *Happiness comes when you focus on what you can give, not what you can get.* It takes persistence, hard work, self-discipline, patience, and most of all, a passion for kids to thrive in your classroom, but the payoff of a fruitful career is well worth what you put into it.

If you find yourself unhappy with your job, then take some time to reflect on why you feel this way. Think about the ideas we have brought up in this chapter, and have some conversations with trusted friends — see what they have to say about who you are and what you do. *We'd be lying if we acted like every person in a classroom today should be there.* Some teachers will never be happy in education because they weren't meant for the job in the first place. Many "fell in love" with an illusion—with their idea of what teaching would be like. *The honeymoon is over.* The only way you are going to make it is if you are in the classroom for the *right* reasons. *If the passion isn't there, none of your preparation will matter.* You have a choice to move on or be miserable. Deciding to leave teaching doesn't mean you are a failure, it simply means your gifts and talents are better invested elsewhere. You owe it to yourself and your students to spend your life the right way.

SUMMARY

I (Scotty) love a wood-burning fireplace. I don't know if it is the smell, the sound, or the testosterone fueling act of conquering the flames, but there is something mesmerizing about a roaring fire burning beneath a mantle. Despite my adoration for the flames, I rarely am able to create the roaring fire of my dreams—my fireplace meows more often than it roars. I know my problem is always the wood. It is usually damp and rotten, mere left-overs from my annual summer backyard bout with mother nature. I am just too cheap to buy real hard wood logs during winter, and too distracted in the summer to stockpile what I always wish I had come December. Thus, winter after winter, I find myself throwing the same old wood into the fire hoping this year's fire will be better than last.

Maybe your career has turned into my fireplace? Your fire may have burned bright in the beginning, but before you can get comfortable on the couch it is barely hanging on and starting to burn out. Your attitude, like my fuel, has become damp and ineffective. Each year you tell yourself that next year is going to be different, but somehow it still seems the same.

Having bad days or a sputtering fire doesn't mean your career is hopeless. It doesn't mean you're a bad teacher. *It means you are a human being.* Let go of the ridiculous notion that life will never interrupt your classroom. When it does—not *if*—don't be discouraged. It is only temporary. Your fire *can* roar again. After all, your troubles may just be the catalyst to alter the future of students going through difficult things themselves (and reminds you why you decided to teach in the first place). Just as I have the power to create the fire of my dreams if I care enough to prepare in advance, *you* have the power to overcome the struggles and stresses that come with being in education and develop into the teacher you always thought you could be. *Don't let the occasional "bad days" turn you into a permanently "bad teacher."* Find the fuel to sustain your fire.

In all honesty, it may be that your fuel cannot be found in the field of education. That's understandable and nothing to be ashamed of. *Sometimes it takes just as much courage to leave education as it does to enter it.* We won't judge you for changing careers (though we may call on summer break and snow days!). Whatever you do with your life, do it with passion and commitment. Your family, your friends, your students, your fireplace, *and you* will be happy that you did.

Mission Impossible

Chapter 14

Engaging passion and purpose, and learning how to leave a legacy

"Mr. Hunt, this isn't mission difficult, it's mission impossible. 'Difficult' should be a walk in the park for you."

- Mission Impossible

It's an iconic scene: Tom Cruise dangles suspended by ultra thin cables from the laser guarded air conditioning vent in the secret vault of C.I.A. headquarters in Langley, Virginia. If the room's temperature rises by more than one degree, he's done. If a bead of sweat falls from his brow onto the motion-detecting floor, he's a goner. If a noise is made higher than a whisper, he's doing time. He has to steal secret files to accomplish his mission, expose the traitor, and salvage his tarnished reputation. *It is a difficult mission to say the least, one might even say it's an impossible mission* — more aptly described as complete and utter insanity.

In a strange sort of way, we think all teachers can relate. You hang suspended by the ultra thin cables of the latest legislation and the ever-evolving curriculum updates safeguarded by the most recent requirements of teacher evaluation protocol in the not so secret classroom of your town, U.S.A. If students do not meet the new benchmarks for mastery, you're done. If the right parent gets rubbed the wrong way, you're a goner. If a student misinterprets one off the cuff remark, you might be doing time. Amidst all of this intensity and pressure, you are forced to attempt your mission: You have to teach your content, manage your classroom, make a difference in the lives of children, protect your (and your school's) reputation, and do it all without getting burned out. *It is a difficult mission to say the least, one might even say it's an impossible mission*—more aptly described as complete and utter insanity.

Ever felt this way? *Every teacher has.* However, as we know all too well, our version is no movie. There is no script, no re-takes, no editing room to cut our mistakes, no computerized special effects, definitely no million dollar paychecks, and no red carpets rolled out as we dart our way through the car loop. *Our mission impossible is real.* The mission is critical, and the odds stacked against us would make even Tom Cruise consider throwing in the towel...

As if teaching weren't hard enough, politicians and educational leadership are calling for bigger and better results over shorter time frames. Schools must have more rigor, more growth, more academics, and less so-called "fluff" (you know, like art, music, physical education, civics, public speaking, economics, technology, electives, character education, culture, finance, vocational skills, and history). Get rid of everything in school that won't boost the results of the next standardized test. No child will be left behind. The promises are grand, the expectations are real, and the cycles of reform are so fast that one initiative has yet to get off the ground before it is replaced with another one.

Who is going to make all this happen? *The teachers, of course.* So let's up the ante and restructure teacher evaluations—we need those to occur more frequently, involve more paperwork, and be all around more strenuous (because most administrators have *tons* of spare time!). Let's raise expectations, standards, accountability, responsibility ...let's raise just about everything except for salaries. There is a lot of push from society but not a lot of support—sort of like promising the performance of a Porsche into the body and budget of a Pinto.

224

Let's not forget the increase of unsupportive parents who seem to do less parenting, yet more complaining; the frightening surge of shootings and violence in schools; and media machines ready to respond with spotlights on any rumor of teacher misconduct. *Whew!* For some strange reason, the low wages, overwhelming workload, emotional toll, lack of parental support, unreasonable expectations, and revolving door of curriculum standards are not attracting and keeping individuals in this profession. As we stated earlier, almost <u>half</u> of new teachers leave the field within five years. *It seems that in recent years, "mission difficult" has turned into "mission impossible"* where the odds of surviving teaching are anything but in our favor.

Okay, we may be exaggerating a bit—there are definitely great perks of being a teacher—but the upsides of teaching aren't enough to keep many from leaving the classroom. In schools all across America, too many teachers just don't make it. They either leave the profession altogether or resign themselves to continue teaching with a sense of mission that doesn't amount to much more than making it to next summer break. *This is a catastrophe of epic proportions.* In the real word, when *teachers* don't succeed—don't accomplish their mission—their *students* don't succeed, which in turn creates a *country* that does not succeed. This is the reality that many people do not realize about educators.

Our career affects everything and everyone in society.

It may sound a bit cliché, but we <u>*are*</u> shaping the future of our nation. Tomorrow's business owners, lawyers, mechanics, professors, scientists, electricians, police officers, politicians, athletes, engineers, murderers, drug dealers, and everything in-between are sitting in our classrooms today. Our leadership, or lack thereof, will help guide them in one direction or another. Obviously parents play a crucial role

225

in the lives of their children, but in today's average American household the reality is that teachers often spend more time shaping children than many parents. *Tomorrow depends on what _teachers_ do today.*

This is it. This is your mission—save the world one student at a time. *Save a world that most likely will never know or acknowledge that you saved it.* Because the reality we face daily as teachers is sort of like the general public in all the Mission Impossible movies—totally oblivious to the fact that the future of life as we know it is teetering on the brink of destruction, and it's up to a handful of us teachers to save the day. What is so incredible about those of us that choose to be difference makers is that we *know* it is "mission impossible." We *know* that we have *every reason* to quit, chase a higher salary, endure less stress, get more respect from society, and eat hour lunches...*but we don't.* We know that we have to fulfill our calling because if we don't, *no one else will.*

You see, it's easy to be a bad teacher, hard to be a good teacher, and almost impossible to be a great teacher...*almost* impossible. *It's the "almost" that will change the future.* It's up to those of us that have the guts to stay in and be more than a mediocre teacher—the elite, the called, the passionate, the ones that didn't quit when the going got tough. Tomorrow is up to all of the *great* teachers, who are *fully aware of the obstacles and odds stacked against them, but determined to make a difference* where it is needed most. Are *you* one of them, or are you merely a survivor drawing a paycheck and counting down the days until summer? You're either in or you're out. Right now. *You have to choose.* You can leave if you want, but if you decide to stay, know that it won't be easy, know that you have to be in it for the right reasons (for them, not you), and then give it all you got. *This is your mission, should you choose to accept it.*

Mission possible

Frodo: *I can't do this, Sam.*

Sam: *I know. It's all wrong. By rights we shouldn't even be here. But we are. It's like in the great stories, Mr. Frodo. The ones that really mattered...those were the stories that stayed with you. That meant something, even if you were too small to understand why. But I think, Mr. Frodo, I do understand. I know now. Folk in those stories had lots of chances of turning back, only they didn't. They kept going. Because they were holding on to something.*

Frodo: *What are we holding onto, Sam?*

Sam: *That there's some good in this world, Mr. Frodo...and it's worth fighting for.*

- The Lord of the Rings (The Two Towers)

What are you holding onto? *How are you going to matter?* The answers to these questions will not be the same for all of us, but teachers must define their purpose and the "mission" of their classroom. Ultimately, teaching should be about something more than mere survival. It should have a *purpose*. To thrive in the classroom, all teachers must define their purpose, their mission. Take time to clarify why it is that you get up in the morning and come to school. What are you doing to help your students thrive? What are you doing that is going to make a better tomorrow?

Besides daily encouragement, another one of my (Scotty) personal missions is to get students to see the connection between *their life* and *their choices*. Because of this goal, I have a large banner hanging in the front of my classroom that reads: *Your Decisions Shape Your Future.* I constantly preach this message to my students.

"Mr. Hicks, do we have to do this project?"

"Mr. Hicks, do we have to read this?"

"Mr. Hicks, do we have to take this test?"

My answer is always the same. "No, you do not, but

your decisions shape your future." I consistently challenge them to live life in "3-D" where <u>D</u>ecisions <u>D</u>etermine <u>D</u>estiny. They can choose to do *or not do* anything in life, but there will always be consequences to those decisions. From this point, in the small world of my classroom, I use consequences (good and bad) to encourage students to make the right decision. It's my hope that the microcosm of Mr. Hicks' room serves as healthy preparation for life outside of public education.

This certainly isn't the singular aim of my classroom, but it is an important one. It's a purpose to my classroom that transcends the latest educational fads, shifts, and legislation. It's a reason that I keep coming into work and a way that I can see my students leave my classroom better than they entered it.

What is *your* mission? What are your reasons for sticking with this crazy profession? It doesn't have to be a long, elaborate statement that you will forget in a few months, but it does have to be genuine and binding. *If you have never taken the time to consider how you will leave your mark on the next generation, then you can be sure that you will not leave a mark at all.* So, take a moment to decide what your classroom, and your students' experience in it, will ultimately be all about.

When you define your mission, your classroom has a unified *purpose* that immediately takes effect. All of a sudden, your students are more than a test score—more than a statistic. All of a sudden, you are more than a teacher evaluation report. All of a sudden, you and your students matter in ways that are much more important than passing an exam. Further still, you will discover that you are chasing something more attainable. You are no longer straining for the impossible goal of advanced content mastery for every single student on the surface of the planet—chasing rhetoric from people who have never taught a day in their life. Remember, a major component of thriving in education is achieving a healthy balance between your classroom and all the other areas of your life. Having a clearly defined mission is part of this plan. It gives you a mission that, though perhaps very difficult, is not impossible...and *it is a mission that is unique and meaningful to you..*

This doesn't mean that everything will be easier, and you can trash your curriculum to teach whatever you want. A sense of mission isn't a magic wand that will make everything in your classroom perfect. You will *still* spend hours creating new lessons, grading a zillion papers, calling a bunch of parents, dealing with students' misbehavior, and second-guessing whether or not teaching is right for you (especially if you are a younger teacher). This is the part in the movie when it appears the bad guy is going to win. *Stay focused, remember your purpose, and don't give up.*

Think of a sports team that makes a goal to win a championship. The coaches will constantly preach to their athletes to "leave it all on the field." This means—do your best, give it all you got, and if you lose, no regrets because you know you didn't hold anything back. Simply deciding to win doesn't make conditioning, practice, scrimmages, and games a piece of cake. It will take dedication, determination, and persistence to accomplish their goal (especially when they lose some games along the way). That being said, having a clearly defined purpose transforms obstacles into hurdles to jump instead of reasons to quit. It will help you to *leave it all in the classroom.*

Taking this analogy one step further, think of yourself as a team member (with other committed teachers) on a mission to make a difference. Just like any sports team, *each player plays a different role in the overall game plan.* You don't have to hit the winning shot to be valuable. You just have to do *your* part and fulfill *your* mission in the grand scheme of things. This frees us to play a crucial role in the lives of kids without carrying the weight of the world on our shoulders.

At the outset of this book, we wrote how Bear Grylls doesn't sit around twiddling his thumbs waiting for someone to come rescue him. He also doesn't use up all of his energy on his first night in the wilderness. He depends on his training, his knowledge, and his available resources to survive in the wild in a way that doesn't kill him in the process. Life is not too different in our classrooms. We can't wait for society to give us the support, salary, and respect we know that we deserve. We must decide whether or not we want to survive or thrive in our classroom—whether or not we want to draw a paycheck or change a child's life. Defining, executing, and pacing your mission are what makes *you* a game-changer. This choice is what makes you part of an elite group that is growing smaller every year because more and more teachers are calling it quits. The buck stops at *your* door. You *can* make a difference. *We all can.*

Legacy vs. Learning

"I have come to believe that a great teacher is a great artist and that there are as few as there are any other great artists. Teaching might even be the greatest of the arts since the medium is the human mind and spirit."
- John Steinbeck

I (Rob) began teaching at my current school very early in my career. When I first started out here, I considered myself to be quite successful. I was young—the "cool" new teacher that all the students wanted. My standardized test scores were high and discipline issues were low so my administration seemed to be in the Mr. Kuban fan club as well. Everything was going great, and my ego was firing on all cylinders. I quickly settled in and began my reign as King of 8th grade Social Studies. Then, *something awful happened.*

230

We hired a new guy. He came from a surrounding district. I sat in on his interview, and despite mentioning that cage fighting was one of his favorite past-times, we hired him (who says something like that when they are trying to get a teaching job!?!). This guy hit the ground running. He was a former soldier—with all kinds of incredible military stories that supplemented his lessons. He evidently opened his class with jokes, video clips, and inspirational stories. I was yesterday's news. It seemed that my illustrious reign had come to an abrupt halt.

Don't get me wrong, I enjoyed working with Scotty and respected him, but admitting someone in the universe might be a better teacher was a bitter pill for my pride to swallow! After getting over the initial shock and adjusting to the much-needed downsizing of my ego, I began to reflect over the differences between our classrooms. I saw a contrast in teaching styles, personalities, and classroom management, but the defining distinction between his class and mine was revealed when I least expected it.

I ran into a girl at a church picnic—the former student of Mr. Hicks that I mentioned a few chapters back. She went on and on about how great he was and how he had changed her life. Driving home and talking to the windshield, I had a sudden epiphany. It clicked. The light bulb went off, and everything made sense. In my classroom, I was focused on *learning*. Scotty was focused on *legacy*. My classroom was centered one hundred and ten percent on learning, curriculum, and content mastery—getting all my students ready to hit it out of the park come time for the big state standardized test. A noble aspiration for sure, but Scotty's classroom, though he certainly did a great job covering the content, was about something *more*.

To put all this into the language we have used in this book—I was a *good* teacher. I had chapters one through ten down to an art. However, when it came to being a *great* teacher, a lot of room remained for improvement. I realized

I was only a great teacher one day out of one hundred and eighty (the day my students took the test). Since then, I have given much thought about what it means to a have a mission in my classroom that is more important than my ego, even more important than mastering curriculum. *I want to be doing something that will matter ten, twenty, thirty years from now.*

It is crucial for every teacher who wants to make a difference to focus on teaching *kids* not just teaching *content*. Think we're exaggerating? Consider this: Do you use the quadratic formula? Can you define "perfect participle?" How many months have thirty-one days? What caused the War of 1812? Can you name the atomic symbol for lead? What is $816 \div 17$ (without using a calculator!)? Now, see how well you can answer these: Which teachers made you feel smart? Which teachers made you feel dumb? Which teachers challenged you? Which teachers bored you to tears? Which teachers taught you something about life? Chances are you had a lot more answers to the second set of questions because legacy often has little to do with learning curriculum. *Legacy is a gift that you give to the next generation.* It's not lesson plans or lectures.

It's you—and how who you are can change who they become.

Obviously all teachers must give due diligence to content mastery and educational instruction, but great teachers go further. *They teach things that are never found on a list of curriculum standards.* These are the difference makers. These are the ones that get remembered. These are the teachers that leave a legacy.

When the last bell rings

Whether you are a survivor, a thriver, or anything in

between, the simple fact remains: Someday the bell will ring, your students will walk out the door, and your career will be over. What will you think about in that moment? *Okay*—after you have sung a chorus of hallelujahs and peeled out of the parking lot—*then* what will you think about? *When you are looking back over your entire career in education, what will matter most?* What will be important when the last bell rings and your last lessons are taught? I (Rob) am inclined to believe that I won't spend retirement thinking about my academic scores, my lesson plans, my evaluations, or my curriculum. I believe I will spend it thinking about *my students.* All the kids I taught—the good, the bad, and everything in between. Did I try to reach them? Did I do my best? Did I make a difference in at least *some* of their lives? Did I stick with it when the going got tough? In a very real way, thinking about what matters most on your last day of work makes a huge difference today. It gives you a perspective that helps you see through the stress and remember what is most important. So again, I ask: *When you leave your classroom for the last time, what will your legacy be?* Leave something behind that matters.

SUMMARY

I AM A TEACHER
I am a teacher, despite what the world thinks of me—
When it envies my days off and laughs at my salary,
I work from 8 to 3:30, home early every night,
One long vacation in the summer, ummm…*yeah right,*
But I am a teacher, and even though I may receive little respect,
It is my students that matter to me, and it is on that which I reflect,
Yes, there have been times that I have barely made it from week to week,
And there have been times that I have stood before my

students too exhausted to speak,
But I do, because…
I am a teacher.

You know they say that those that can't…teach,
Well I say that very few can…teach,
Very few can put on an encouraging smile even when they
are tired,
Very few have the ability to motivate and inspire,
To challenge every child regardless of the strength of their
mind,
To make them grow as a student and feel strong inside,
Who else can make a child feel pride, when their family at
home doesn't even care if they are alive?
Well I can, because…
I am a teacher.

I am part of an elite group that builds dreams,
Coaches young ones to swim upstream,
And teaches outcasts to work on a team,
I build character, have expectations that are high,
And I make my students learn even though they may
whine,
I AM A TEACHER!

And I was called to what I do,
I make a difference in this world — *How about you?*
I have shed a lot of sweat and tears on my classroom floors,
All for the students that walk through those doors,
And fortunately for this world, there are many more of me,
And fortunately for this world, *I chose to teach.*

Why did *you* choose to teach? It was about *something
more* than content wasn't it? It was about something *much
deeper* than summers off right? It was a calling —*a mission*—
an incredibly difficult, but life-changing, meaningful, and
possible mission.

Reclaim your mission impossible.

Teaching never has been and never will be for the faint of heart. It is for real men and women bent on making a difference in this world. They won't be featured on magazine covers or found with bulging bank accounts. They won't be followed by the paparazzi or by millions on Twitter. But, great teachers *will* change the future. They *will* change the lives of children. *They* will be remembered *long after* the people whose faces are on magazines and whose bank accounts are bulging. *They* will be remembered *long after* the person chased by a paparazzi or creating a buzz on Twitter. *They trade today's glory for tomorrow's greatness.*

When teaching about Abraham Lincoln, I (Rob) always like to point out to my students a very ironic line in the Gettysburg Address: "The world will little note, nor long remember what we say here." In the most famous speech in American history, Abraham Lincoln humbly stated that he didn't think anyone was ever going to remember what he said...*but they did*. They did because his message mattered. They did because he spoke with conviction and purpose. They did because he stood up in the middle of a war and reminded everyone what they were fighting for. They did because his message inspired thousands to honor those who had gone before them by finishing what they started and creating a new tomorrow for the next generation. They did because he gave hope to those that had none. That, my fellow teachers, is what teaching is all about.

Your mission should you choose to accept it is...
Don't settle for educational survival. *Thrive.* Find your passion and purpose, and teach like the future of our world depends on what you do every day...because it does!

[This book will self-destruct in thirty seconds.]

Final Word

-- EXIT CARD --

1. Will you lead or leave your classroom?

2. Will you choose to rise above mediocrity?

3. What will be your legacy?

4. Rate this book on a scale of 1-10.
   (Circle answer below)

   10   10   10   10   10   10   10   10   10   10

So you think you can teach?

We are teachers *just like you*. We have ups, downs, and everything in between. We haven't tamed the wilderness of American education, but we do our best to make a difference because we care. Some days we believe our efforts are making the world a better place, and we have other days when we feel like the best way to make the world a better place is to launch a few students to a galaxy far, far away! Some days we know we are having an impact, and other days, much like Abraham Lincoln, we think no one will ever remember what we say and do. We are teachers just like you.

We wrote this book to guide educators in their journey through the vast and often uncharted territory of being a teacher. It is our humble hope that you will use this information to survive, arrive, and thrive in *your* classroom. In fact, we would love to hear your thoughts and unique experiences from your own voyage. Please connect with us on our website:

howtosurviveteaching.com

Or email us:
howtosurviveteaching@gmail.com

Thriving teachers are needed now more than ever. You <u>can</u> become one. <u>*You*</u> *can* make a difference, and when you do, tell us about it! As you well know, *everyone that has ever taught could write a book on education*...which is exactly where we would like to finish things off.

So you think *you* can teach? Think *you* know something about surviving and thriving in education? *We think you do,* and we want to hear your thoughts. *If you are out there day in and day out succeeding in your classroom, then we <u>know</u> you have your own secrets — your own expertise.* You don't have to have a graduate degree, an office, a title, or even tenure. *You just need to have a classroom.* You aren't required to be a department head, a committee chair, or a representative at the latest summit. *All you have to be is a teacher.* We think that any teacher getting it done in a classroom deserves to be heard.

We want to give you a platform to share your hard-earned advice and receive the same from others. *Our vision is to create a network of real teachers helping other real teachers.* Not a network focusing on lesson plans or curriculum like most educational websites (there are <u>millions</u> of these already), but one where dedicated teachers share personal and pertinent experiences, advice, and stories to assist and inspire other teachers (or at least give them a good laugh!). Not a cyber-soapbox where everyone rants about the stresses of education (like some strange Internet version of a faculty lounge), but a positive and uplifting environment that will push us all a little closer to thriving in this profession.

Our goal is to unleash the expertise bound up in schools all across the country. We don't know what it will look like yet (we are in the developmental phase of several ideas), but we do know that *those of us in the trenches deserve a place to be heard and helped by other educators.* We want you to feel like there's a supportive community of teachers who value and respect what you bring to the table...just a few clicks away. If you are interested in being a part of this, then simply send us an email:

howtosurviveteaching@gmail.com
Put "I am an educational expert" in the subject line.

Join our dream of creating a way for *teachers to inspire teachers* and make the most of their calling. After we receive your email, we will officially grant you the title of *"Educational Expert."* Who knows, you might even get a raise!?! Okay, not really, but we still want to hear from you!

[We hope you read all of this in less than thirty seconds.]

...25...26...27...28...29...

HowToSurvive Teaching.com

howtosurviveteaching@gmail.com

**HowToSurvive
Teaching.com**

howtosurviveteaching@gmail.com

HowToSurvive Teaching.com